COMUS

A Dialogic Mask
by
John Kinsella

COMUS

A Mask
by
John Milton

2008

Published by Arc Publications
Nanholme Mill, Shaw Wood Road
Todmorden OL14 6DA, UK
www.arcpublications.co.uk

Copyright © John Kinsella 2008
Design by Tony Ward
Printed in Great Britain by
the MPG Books Group, Bodmin and King's Lynn

978 1906570 23 1 (hbk)

ACKNOWLEDGEMENTS

The Publishers would like to thank Richard Axton for his assistance in checking the original Milton version and Tim Cribb for his invaluable advice throughout the project.

The version of Milton's *Comus* reproduced in this volume has been taken from the text published in 1645.

This book is in copyright. Subject to statutory exception and to provision of relevant collective licensing agreements, no reproduction of any part of this book may take place without the written permission of Arc Publications.

The Publishers acknowledge financial assistance from ACE Yorkshire

*To the Cambridge University
Marlowe Dramatic Society*

Contents

Tim Cribb – 'Sabrina dear': an introduction / 9

John Kinsella – Comus: A Dialogic Mask / 21

John Milton – Comus: A Mask / 71

John Kinsella – My *Comus*, Milton's *Comus*: an afterword / 120

Biographical notes / 127

'Sabrina dear': an introduction
Tim Cribb

Milton's court masque was commissioned by John, Earl of Bridgewater. It was to be part of the revels to celebrate his inauguration as President of the Council of Wales – in effect a viceroy, with his own court – and it was presented at Ludlow Castle, his administrative headquarters, at the beginning of the autumn in 1634. The Earl must also have commissioned, at the very least by approval, the topic for the masque – chastity. It was a courageous, indeed confrontational choice, for it can only have re-opened a wound inflicted on his family honour three summers before. In May 1631 the Earl's brother-in-law had been executed for allegedly procuring and committing rape and sodomy on the Earl's own step-sister, his twelve-year old step-niece, and on various servants. The confrontation with this shame was designed to cure it, for that is what masques did, at least in theory. As Stephen Orgel expounds in *The Illusion of Power* (1975): 'They teach, they celebrate virtue, they persuade by example; they lead the court to its ideal self' (p. 57). They worked on two levels: vices were impersonated by professional players in an antimasque, and were dispelled when the courtiers themselves stepped forward in a dance; sin, error and illusion gave way to their real-life superiors. The Earl's two young boys, the Brothers in Milton's masque, had appeared in just such a display at Whitehall earlier in the year, *Coelum Britannicum*, perhaps the most lavish of all such celebrations by the court of Charles I of its own virtues.

If that is what a masque does, then, given the particular topic, young John Milton was just the man to write it. In

1628 he too had been courageous and confrontational about chastity. Some of his fellow students at Christ's had nicknamed him "Domina", "Lady", alluding to his fair skin and chaste behaviour. Milton's response is most interesting, both in what he says and when he says it. He doesn't so much deny as, by embracing, transcend the terms and assumptions by which he is taunted. Anticipating T. S. Eliot, he compares himself with Tiresias, who was changed into a woman, or to the nymph Caenis, who was raped by a god, then rewarded for the dishonour by being changed into a man (the ironies multiply), or has he been transformed by some witch of Thessaly (an allusion to Apuleius implying that perhaps he is now an ass)? He concedes that because of his fair skin he may not look like a farmhand, but that doesn't mean he has to prove his manhood by binge drinking or going to the brothel. To be called too little the man can even be an honour and he would rather be called a Dionysian singing girl than be bereft of the Muses. These learnèd allusions play confidently across the stereotypes of gender expectation to wittily confusing effect. The allusion to Dionysus is particularly interesting, given the occasion, for Milton takes the opportunity to make his riposte when presiding in College Hall as Father of Misrule at one of those end-of-term festive occasions from which dons tactfully withdraw. It was a "Salting", like an American fraternity hazing, a student rite of passage in which competitors had to drink salted beer as penalty for losing. Milton is himself the ambiguously gendered Dionysus in charge, but a Dionysus transvalued by that extraordinary combination of Protestant reform with idealising Renaissance Humanism that animates so many Elizabethan writers, not least Milton's poetic maestro, Spenser. At the age of nineteen, Milton thus demonstrates that he's at the cutting edge of mythopoetic thinking, which is what enables him to embrace the role of entertainer with such aplomb. That thinking included the Baconian and magian science of his day, whose triumphs are correctly prophesied in another of his vacation exercises: 'The spirit of man... will reach out far and wide, till it fills the whole world, and the space far beyond... He will indeed seem to be one whose rule and dominion the stars obey...; to whom... Mother Nature herself has surrendered'. He shows the same confidence three years later when commissioned to write for a state instead of merely student occasion.

His bold stroke now is to turn masqueing itself into a sort of anti-masque by inventing the figure of Comus, for that name comes from the Greek word κῶμος, a revel (in *The Birth of Tragedy* Nietzsche translates it as *rausch*, intoxication, ecstasy). In Milton's working manuscript at Trinity, he drafts various stage directions for the entry of Comus's troupe, clearly still with gender-ambiguity in mind: 'their garments some like men's and some like women's they come on in a wild and humorous antic fashion / intrant κωμαζοντες [revelling]. To dramatise celebration as a character in its own performance shows a metatheatrical daring similar to that in the *Bacchae*, where Euripides brings androgynous Dionysus on stage as an actor in his own religious festival. (Milton had purchased his own edition of Euripides that year.)

This puts the audience in an uneasy relation with the occasion and the medium. Have they gathered together to celebrate an inauguration or is celebration itself in question? The pleasure of entertainment is rendered ambivalent and unstable. When the scene changes from the dark wood to Comus's brightly-lit and stately palace, the audience would have expected that they were moving from anti-masque into the masque proper, from darkness to light, from uncouth nature to high culture; but the lavish banquet turns out to be a trap, so the expectations are not merely disappointed but questioned. Again, since in the Whitehall masque it is the king or his aristocratic representative who steps forward to dispel the anti-masque and resolve the issues, so in Ludlow the audience would have expected the Earl to do the same, but instead it is Sabrina. After she has released the Lady, the children are simply presented to their father by their music teacher. In contrast to the masques at Whitehall, the action of Milton's ends on a sobering downbeat of realism, looking to the future and further education, just like his other major poems.

True, at this point the Earl and his lady will doubtless have risen from their seats to join their children and 'Triumph in victorious dance / Ore sensual Folly and Intemperance', but their dance is framed by two others. Immediately preceding it is the country dance by the locals, and although this yields place to the dance of the nobly born, that too yields when the Spirit announces his return to a yet higher court 'Up in the broad fields of the sky', where 'Revels the spruce and jocond Spring'. All human revels, whether rustic or courtly and including those of a κῶμος are but aspirations to or versions and perversions of those. It is ultimately the dance in heaven and the ability of the human spirit to rise up through nature to join it that underpins the confidence with which different and opposing elements in the text, its words, allusions and characters, are implicated in each other, not least Comus and the Attendant Spirit. Both are daemons (the latter so-called in the Trinity manuscript), both sublunary, though higher and lower in Nature. They echo each other visually – for both disguise as shepherds – and in their actions: at the Lady's first entrance, Comus dismisses his rout with 'Break off, break off, I feel the different pace / Of som chaste footing'; at her last entrance, the Attendant Spirit interrupts the rustic dance with 'Back, Shepherds, back, enough your play'. The good and the bad, disorderly riot and honest country dance, are woven into each other as part of the dynamism of life itself. The conclusive resolutions of the Whitehall masques are unrealistic; Renaissance metaphysics teaches that Comus will always escape, for he is part of life.

That is why the Earl's sons, however valiant or noble, cannot free their sister; nor, even, can the Attendant Spirit – but at least he knows there is another way: Sabrina. She originates in the medieval historian, Geoffrey of Monmouth, but he merely tells the story of how the Severn got its name from the drowning there of an historical character, Sabrina. History had to be worked on by the alchemy of Renaissance mythopoesis to reveal its higher meaning and that is what Spenser had begun to do in his Romance, where, according to Milton, 'more is meant than meets the ear'. Spenser set the incident in a genealogy of the Virgin Queen, tracing her ancestry back to Trojan Brutus, thus conferring modern meaning on ancient history. Drayton had followed up by making the personified Severn a major character running through five books of his poetic chorography of Britain's rivers, *Poly-Olbion*. It is when tracing the source of the Severn and her sister Wye from Plinlimmon that he celebrates ancient Druid wisdom in poetry, the haughty pride in arms of the Welsh, and attacks those who restrict history to mere fact, whereas, he argues, it has always been the case 'where wit hath found / A thing most clearly true, it made that fiction's ground' (VI, 291-92). It is then Milton who elevates the story of Sabrina to its full potential as myth, a myth of chastity. He thus brings to bear on his commission from the Earl the highest cultural resources of the Renaissance. The Lady and the family honour are rescued by poetry.

If poetry is the key, then in John Kinsella's dialogue with Milton, who is Sabrina? Well, to begin with, you won't find her in the pages of a medieval historian. Kinsella gives her a more impeccably pastoral genealogy than does Milton, for the Spirit has heard about her directly from a local shearer. Moreover, when we learn that she threw herself into the Severn, it is not she who metamorphoses into a nymph but the river which surprisingly relocates, for she's rescued by a bunch of girls who are 'strong swimmers all' – girls you are far more likely to come across in the Avon of South Western Australia than in the chillier waters of the Avon that flows into the Severn. Milton's Severn is a liminal zone of transition running through the Welsh Marches, between the natural and the supernatural; in Kinsella's masque that zone has expanded to a liminality that encompasses the UK and the Antipodes as globalized commodity transactions implicate one place within another. The girls are in a 'local coven', simultaneously both New Age hippy drop-outs in Oz and traditional Welsh witches. The beautiful neoplatonic translucency of nature which is the medium of Milton's goddess translates, through Sabrina's political conversion into an eco-warrior, into 'the clear and present danger / MI5 says she is today'. When Milton's Spirit adds 'the power of som adjuring verse' to summon her, he calls on the mythological deities who inhabit the waters, beginning with Neptune. These are the names of power in Renaissance poetics so this is the passage in Milton's text where they crowd in most densely. Kinsella too resorts to the list form in its most solemn version, invocation, but dispenses with the gods, returning to an Adamic simplicity: first come the landscapes; these are then animated by the creatures; in either case named only as themselves.

When Sabrina finally rises, the quality of her persona is instantly captured in the first line of her song: 'I hope to show'. She is the Fairy Godmother of pantomime, ditzy and *distrait* but loveable with it. Rather as Fairy Godmothers tend to get entangled in their accoutrements and have trouble making their spells work, Sabrina's song is cluttered up with all the things she wants to keep out of it, the effluent pipes and phone towers and fertilisers. Her vague attempts to wave them away are plainly ineffectual: 'No need for motor boats or cars', 'Let the stoats hunt and the squirrels forage', and she can only conclude her breathless logic with 'And so... at your request / I am here'. The Spirit, sounding like Buttons in a fix, greets her in the same generic, already cod, theatrical idiom:

> Sabrina dear
> we beg you to use your power
> to undo the bonds that skewer
> this virgin to this device;
> she was trapped here
> by an unethical bio-engineer.

Terrific fun, you may say, but, at this crisis in the action, what's happened to Poetry when we need it?

The answer lies in all those things that have got into Sabrina's song, for it's our song too. All of us feed on fertilised food, are consequently connected to nature by effluent pipes, and to each other via phone towers. Hence these words and others like them, coined by science and applied through technologies, clatter through our speech and our newspapers. The words of Mercury may seem harsh after the songs of Apollo, but there's no living, or dying, without them. They seem harsh because in the past Apollo's songs have been based on what were the iambic rhythms of English speech. But the rhythms of speech in English have changed, not only according to different national locations, but because one of the vectors of its internationalisation is science, which is the same in all locations. It is the language of science and technology which has multiplied the number of throwaway syllables in modern speech. The ending of the word "technology" itself, for example, is incorrigibly dactylic, and in a pentameter line can only sound like a mouthful of gabble. But it's in the midst of this gabble that Kinsella, renewing Wordsworth's attempt to use 'the real language of men', pitches his tent. He is thus able to accommodate, without change to the speaking voice of ordinary modern conversation, Milton's own science in a way very different from Milton. Compare:

> That's not why they persecuted Galileo
> and his vitality of science. A science
> that co-exists with forests. Listen....

with

> Hung on his shoulders like the Moon, whose Orb
> Through Optic Glass the *Tuscan* Artist views
> (*Paradise Lost*, I, 288)

The one we could hear at any dinner-table conversation in Cambridge or Perth; the other only in iambic verse. In *Disclosed Poetics* (2007) Kinsella quotes another Australian poet, Robert Adamson, who cites the prediction of the American poet, Robert Creeley: 'Your subject will arise out of the language' (p. 96).

This fidelity to speech is not to say that Kinsella merely mimes modern usage, not even sardonically (although that tone is available when wanted). The comedy of Sabrina testifies to a freedom of spirit going beyond reproduction or rancour, and it is a freedom created by poetry. If you write out the first sentence of Kinsella's masque and ignore the line breaks you will produce a passage of truly dreadful prose. The links between the clauses are so loosely articulated by participles and appositions that the sentence gets lost in its own length and rambles on, to use its own words, in 'haphazard agglomeration'. This is indeed mimetic, since ordinary speech does ramble, so it's a kind of realism; as such it functions as characterisation. But supervening on this are the interruptions of the line breaks, and the same looseness that serves to define the variables of character is converted into an asset of a different order when the line breaks are restored. For as you come to the end of a line, a space opens out beyond the last word, leaving it suspended for a fraction of a beat as the eye and the voice move to the beginning of the next line. The last word is given space to acquire a resonance of its own, or of the space's own. You cannot read past the word for the meaning anticipated by the syntax, as you would in prose, where the word is made merely instrumental to a discourse pursuing its own purpose. The word enters into a kind of dialogism with the character and even with the poet. The speaker may pursue whatever may be their line of thought, their foibles or obsessions, but the word is liberated from that discursive intent and hovers in its own dimension of meaning. Hence, to adapt Milton on Romance, the ear hears more than is meant by the speaker. A wonderful instance of this is the very first line of Kinsella's masque: 'Before the difficult skies of Science', where the last word is set free to reverberate through the whole poem, pre-empting any possibility of discursive limitation.

This effect is not limited to the ends of the lines. The line length that enables the breaks is in itself arbitrary. It derives from two sources. The first is the intervals of phrasing as they occur in modern speech. These yield a wide variation of line-length but with a median of seven syllables and three stresses. That converges with Milton's practice when he shortens the pentameter to a mixture of tetrameters and trimeters in order to speed up the dionysiac passages of his masque. The seven-syllable median thus becomes part of Kinsella's dialogue with Milton, so that occasionally the two poems can exactly coincide; both Comuses dance 'In a light fantastic round'. The lineation is thus grounded both in literary tradition and modern speech. It is the play of the latter over the arbitrary line length that creates the caesuras, and these can occur at any point in the line into which the phrasing has run over. Thus the caesuras, like the line-endings, come to the rescue of the prosy ramblings of the speakers by setting words reverberating in a space beyond their immediate context. This makes for a Modernist, post-Mallarméan verse-drama. The Modernism is more Joycean than Mallarméan in that it works through parody, although that shouldn't distract from the haunting darkness of lines like 'peeling back the tepid / light', the menacing grandeur of 'revelling in the mortality of stars', or the pathos of 'thinking over residues of pastoral, / singing quietly of the old ways'. But these are relatively easy to hear. Actors of the masque will also need to call on a less directly expressive, more Brechtian technique to capture subtle effects of estrangement within the comedy. The challenge to the actors is to deliver to the audience not just the character or even the topic but what Kinsella might call 'the pre-uttered poem' beyond them.

The continuities between the two masques and their writers are thought-provoking. Both masques are written to commission, both are for performance on ritualised occasions for revelling and inversions: the feast of St. Michael and all Angels that inaugurates Michaelmas Term and all magistrates in the former case; May Week and the rites of passage from university to the world beyond in the second. Indeed, Kinsella's masque was commissioned for performance in the very College Hall where the student Milton presided as Father of Misrule. Both writers are keenly committed to avant-garde thinking, including science: in his most recent volume, *Shades of the Sublime and Beautiful*, Kinsella goes as far as any current poet I know in furthering Wordsworth's ambition of 'carrying sensation into the midst of the objects of Science'. Both writers are radical reformers, the first a republican regicide, the other a vegan anarchist. But the strongest bond between them is their fidelity to Sabrina.

COMUS
A Dialogic Mask
JOHN KINSELLA

THE PERSONS
   The Attendant Spirit
      afterwards in the habit of Thyrsis
   Comus with his crew
   The Lady
   Elder Brother
   Second Brother
   Sabrina the Nymph

First performed in June 2008 at Christ's College, Cambridge, by Christ's College Amateur Dramatic Society in conjunction with Cambridge University Marlowe Society to celebrate the 400th anniversary of John Milton's birth.

THE CAST
   The Attendant Spirit – Helen Duff
   Comus – David Brown
   The Lady – Amanda Palin
   Elder Brother – Sam Pallis
   Second Brother – Lowri Amies
   Sabrina – Alashiya Gourdes
   Entourage – Abigail Rokison, Iona Blair, Arthur Asseraf

   Composer – Simon Gethin Thomas
   Musical Adviser – Jeremy Thurlow
   Designer – Lucy Minyo   Associate Designer – Georgia de Grey
   Lighting Designer – Ben Sehovic
   Technical Director – Adam Wood
   Stage Manager – Alexandra Hepburn
   Producer – Pascal Porcheron   Associate Producer – Eve Rosato
   Director – Simon Godwin   Assistant Director – Oscar Toeman

The first scene set in a Wild Wood.

The Attendant Spirit descends or enters.

Before the difficult skies of Science
my forest is, where species
verging on extinction live protected,
in a region of clean and serene air,
beyond the dismal smoke and emptiness
people call Earth, trapped in their
cycle of plasma greenery, worship
of cars and technology, imprisoning
us in our nature, fighting to live
as we have lived, die also, unconcerned
with benefits meted out by the self-
empowered, self-rewarding, self-
congratulating, to the forest alone
I admit eternity, to the haphazard
agglomeration of atoms and molecules
a pattern, a design, a beauty: I would not
despoil this for all the profits of progress.
      But to my task. God observing
every destructive particle of salt, each
failing stream, sought the upper atmosphere
to find a paradox: thin and choking; and below,
the sea heavier than metal, necrotic
tides dragging against the force
of the moon, the deep a trash compressor,

flensed of pressure for all to see:
the need, the lack of restraint, make
for a strange democracy, let the privileged
wield their little tridents, this Isle
in the thick of it: now, from the North Sea
to the deepest oils of Antarctica,
down past the colonies where independence
was atomic testing in the Montebellos,
Maralinga… even a Prime Minister
sacked like republic wherever the pink
of industry reached. So war
strikes at the heart of forests.
And so they burn year in year out,
throwing a pall over the equator:
we enjoy that rainforest-timber finish:
aesthetics: and so our children mix ecology
with machinery, seeing neither
as mutually exclusive: a perplexing
path of "sustainability", the horror
of genetics and history, the measuring
up, the quantifying, turning observation
to military-industrial sovereignty.
That's not why they persecuted Galileo
and his vitality of science. A science
that co-exists with forests. Listen,
and I will tell you now, a cybernetic
folktale. The young brothers you see
wandering here don't recognise

their defence at hand: landscape.
It is the silver of the scientist
they should consider carefully.
    Bacchus, party boy, purveyor
of ecstasy, sailed out through the city
bars and nightclubs, cruising until
his mates dumped him at a club
whose five pounds entry belied
the true cost of enchantment.
There he fell to exquisite Circe,
daughter of the Sun, swine-maker,
who bent the rules to have sex
with this dreadlocked youth,
delivering of him a Son, much like
his father, but even more like his mother,
whom she raised in the club and named Comus,
who ambitious, and exuberant in his majority,
roved the Irish and British fields,
at last arriving at the bounty of this forest,
inculcating himself deep in its shadows,
outdoing his mother in her genetic arts,
offering to every passerby his elixir,
a patented offering that would
bring eternal youth, slimness, a larger
penis. Soon as the formula ran its course,
they transformed into some artificial life:
resembling Wolf or Bear or Tiger or Hog
or Bearded Goat, but with no before,

no configuring through family or birth.
Their bodies remained as they'd been,
and yet small vestige of the human remained.
And lament their loss? Far from it!
They strutted and bragged, sure
the product had enhanced their strength
and beauty! Where they'd travelled before
they forgot, and ranting through days
of methamphetamine and ecstasy,
raved and raged: twenty-four hour
party people trashing the forest.
So when any enters with a love
of the woods and not the chemicals
they might extract, I shoot down faster
than starlight and give them safe passage.
As I do now: but first I must lose
this *haute couture* and look as hired help
of an upper-income house, who with his
iPod and smooth moves, swings
through the forest as if it's his day off,
all the leaves bending to my beat,
an extension of nature. A flower child
slipped out of its era. Retro-chic. Classless.
But I hear the grind of evil. I am transparent!

> *Comus enters with a wand in one hand, his glass in the*
> *other; with him a rout of monsters headed like sundry sorts*
> *of wild beasts, but otherwise like men and women, their*

apparel glistering, making a riotous and unruly noise, with burning brands in their hands.

Comus
The satellite is in place,
and the dull day's race
is run, time for the sun
to set and our night fun
to commence – pole dancers,
strippers, fanciers
of orgies and bondage,
come on, rage, rage
with the dying of the light,
praise wrong over right,
fart and breed,
spill your seed,
turn flesh to medicine,
frontiers are never sin.
Midnight frenzy,
dance and jollity.
Good sense has retired,
yet with good sense we've conspired,
we've narrowed the gap,
we've sucked the marrow from the ape,
Huntingdon Life Sciences
rises lustily from the fires.
New scientists are horny cunts
and the nay-sayers nasty runts,

moaning on about the lower
ranks – dogs, cats, and lower
still. What pathetic people
would cry over mice, scruple
over the fate of a rat,
hippies with a brat
at the breast, greenies
who are terrorists.
What is night to do with sleep?
Night has better things to reap.
Sex is on the cards,
let's trounce their communards –
it's only transparency
and accountability
that are loss, in darkness
we divest and undress
this forest: hail all secret deals,
all government steals,
all pacts with private industry,
all religious duplicity,
all litterers and miners,
all timber merchants and farmers:
no matter how much they doom
it remains dark as a dragon's womb,
as the trees go the air
thickens with despair,
so fuck the sun
and fuck their Luddite fun,

let's beat the ground
in a light fantastic round.

The measure.

Enough, enough, something has shifted,
some innocent feet approach.
Quickly, enshroud yourselves
in the tinsel and glitter of plantation trees,
as our crowd will frighten away
the virgin I sense nearby.
Now to my prowess and a dose
of Viagra. Soon I will own a herd
as busy as that of my mother Circe.
And so I throw my spells to the market,
I trial my formula: power to cheat
the eye with bare illusion,
and give it false presentments; lest
the trappings of my habitat
give the wrong impression – that my science
is the benefit of humanity and the forest,
and send the girl I sense, I taste, to flight,
I'd best put on the manners of a debonair
scientist, or one naive of his brilliance,
or one too consumed to care or notice
her alluring wares. When her eye
has been doused in this barbiturate,
I shall appear as some harmless hippy

who can only afford rags and sandals.
But here she comes, hot as…
Let me step aside and listen
to her confession.

The Lady enters.

I am pretty sure the noise came from here,
if my ears didn't deceive me; it sounded
like a rave, a gate-crashed party
where strangers have run amok,
neighbourhood dogs all worked up
and barking in a frenzy,
as if possessed by Pan himself.
It's not my scene – give me quiet
coffee with friends anytime –
but where else can I go
in this tangled, entombing forest?
My brothers, restless at their age,
left me stretched out reflecting
beneath these pines, saying
they'd fetch me sweet berries
from a thicket just out of sight.
And then evening was suddenly
upon me, peeling back the tepid
light, immersing my sense of sight.
Where on earth are they? Why
haven't they returned? Typical…

I guess they wandered too far
and dark caught them out,
stealing them from me, O evil night
shutting down even the light
of the night sky, blocking nature out,
revelling in the mortality of stars,
why did you disorient the traveller?
I am here now, I think, where the noise
writhed and ceased, rife yet perfect
in my ear... yet darkness is all that's
here... and only a sense of the uncanny
lives: shapes form out of shadow,
shadow whispers, and the language
of aloneness and abandonment
is sibilant as sands and shores the vast
cleared spaces of the dustbowl world,
crackling with its dry breath.
But I have hope, and within the folds
of darkness the forest persists,
breathes, informs and transforms
itself like an angel of gold wings.
A chastity. A holding back.
I see it visibly. Not all things
need be torn open. Protesters
locked on against the police, the company.
Does the light of a communal fire
throw a silver lining on the night?
I cannot call my brothers,

but am emboldened in my campaign
to call against this unnatural darkness.
Perhaps they are close by.

SONG

Sweet echo, static of the era
    collapsing biosphere
  by the clotting river,
within the threatened wood
    where the forlorn bird
sings elegies for all that disappear.

    Can't you tell me of a gentle pair
      who like Narcissus are?
        If you have
    hidden them in a dank cave,
      only tell me where
sweet echo, ring of bright water,
  so you might translate the skies
and restore country's damaged harmonies.

COMUS
Could any sex doll be cast
that would promise such indulgence?
There's something pure in that flesh
that shakes this fetid air,
that betrays its residence;

her words break through raven night,
fill its rookery with delight
until each beak turns up in a smile.
I have heard my mother Circe
with the Sirens and research assistants
making medicines and testing drugs
that bring a smile before decline,
singing lifestyle ads on television
while imprisoning souls,
bending agencies to their wish,
wining and dining department heads,
profiting from the vanity of universities,
but such a sacred and home-felt delight,
such sobriety and certainty of bliss
I haven't heard till now. She's
the one for me. We shall be
the power couple of the dailies.
Maybe there's a touch of outsider
about her? That would explain it.
New blood for the throne. My party
will call it a dirty little secret, but hey,
it's time we moved on. The new rurality.
A prosperous wedding of interests.

LADY
Gentle farmhand, I am sorry for yelling
and sending those echoes ringing
through the woods, my call wasn't

intended for you – I am searching
for company and needs must…

COMUS
How did you lose them?

LADY
Through darkness and this labyrinthine forest.

COMUS
Surely they should have stuck close by you given night?

LADY
They went off in search of greener places…

COMUS
They treated you with disdain?

LADY
No, no… to find fresh fruit to feed me…

COMUS
And left you unprotected?

LADY
The two of them intended to be back in a flash…

Comus
Hmmm... yes, night could have disturbed them...

Lady
It is terrible luck...

Comus
You are worried about them aside?

Lady
To lose two brothers!

Comus
They were youths or men?

Lady
Neither has begun to shave.

Comus
I did come across two as you describe,
around the time the cows were being
brought in from the fields that surround
these woods: I saw them beneath
the green vine that winds its way
along the small hill on the wood's edge,
plucking ripe clusters; they looked unearthly
in that unformed light, as if drawn
from a rainbow through the clouds.

I prayed to them as spirits: heaven
is close to the ground in these parts.

LADY
Farmhand, could you tell me how to find them?

COMUS
Head west from this overgrown spot.

LADY
To track them in this night of absent starlight,
would be testing my skills. I haven't got my phone
on me – pity, it has an inbuilt global positioning system.

COMUS
Technography is in my waters – all farmers
know their science these days. I know
every nook and cranny, every cable
planted below our feet, every tower
emitting microwaves in this vicinity.
I possess nomenclature… epistemology.
I know the co-ordinates of my walk,
I know the gene that awakes
fields of rape, warm weather plants
that thrive in cold, the pig that is vaccine.
This is the morphology of the country.
Let me take you to my place,
a modern dwelling in which you'll be safe.

LADY
Thanks, kind farmhand, I appreciate
the offer – in truth, workers
are more likely to share their bounty,
their travel shots from abroad
and cans of lager, their aspirations
for Man City rather than Chelsea,
than the wealthy who dwell
in designer towers or revamped
manors, replete with wireless
technology and grand facades.
I will follow you happily.

The two Brothers

ELDER BROTHER
It's mayhem here: moon, pierce
the clouds and illuminate these warped
woods of doubled darkness, or if shadows
have you wrapped in self-pity,
send a dart of light through some hole,
tear apart the mists, enlighten us
and you shall be our star of Arcady.

SECOND BROTHER
Or if our eyes be denied such happiness,
let us hear the sheep in their pens,
progeny of Dolly, short-lived

and straining against the pasture,
or a whistle from the house
(designed by the architects
who enamoured Canary Wharf),
or a chorus of battery hens –
it would be of some solace,
some pleasure in this dungeon
of "nature". But where is our
sister, a virgin wandering
out here in the cold, vulnerable
to burrs and thistles?
Perhaps she is using some cold bank
as a pillow, or is wrapped
in elm-bark, wild with fear?
Or as we speak gripped hard
by savage hunger or savage heat?

ELDER BROTHER
Relax, brother – don't be so enthusiastic
to deconstruct the fashion of dubious evils:
why avoid evil and pursue it at the same time?
And if it's just the manufacture of fear,
self-delusion will just lead you astray.
And don't seek my sister thinking that,
as I know her well enough in my own way.
She's not one who driving on a highway
would swerve to strike a snake,
get her thrills from killing

what she fears. I don't think she
is in danger – I hope not, and though
the absence of light and noise might
disturb her inner peace, if she listens
again she will hear a radiant light
of the unaltered living life at night.
The solitude of wildness offsets
the terror of bodies dumped,
crimes committed out of sight,
the developer's survey markers
dividing the body up: an orgy
of divvying, a clearing to replant.
Her best nurse is contemplation,
and maybe time away from those
who'd *guide* her, might let an inner light
spread out brighter than a bright day:
to lurk within a dark soul
is night at midday.
We can only make
our own dungeons.

SECOND BROTHER
There's something to be said
for the hermit buried in the woods,
smoking weed and counting beads,
drinking from a maple dish
and stroking a grey beard.
What do thought and meditation

have in common? Silently,
they break the door down
of the private cell – she lives
in fear though she hides it.
I tell you, her smoothness
needs protecting by those
who would not seek advantage,
defend her fruit from the lascivious:
I have seen this place in dirty dvds
our patron has left around…
You can't convince me it's safe,
you see it on TV everyday:
danger will give the nod
to opportunity, and leave me
little hope a young woman
would pass through these wastes
safely; I fear neither night
nor loneliness, but I fear
what they will bring our sister.

ELDER BROTHER
I wasn't suggesting, brother,
that our sister was safe
beyond all doubt, but I am
optimistic by nature.
Furthermore, our sister
is not without resilience,
and is stronger than you

seem to remember.

SECOND BROTHER
What strength outside
her religious convictions
do you mean?

ELDER BROTHER
Yes, she has religious conviction
but conviction doesn't work alone:
she desires her purity – her virginity
encases her in steel… and this makes
her as deadly as a bullet from a rifle,
and all the contents of forest, heath, and hills,
bend to her will, and no deviant
would dare degrade her: she will
pass by safely before every cleft
and rocky outcrop, each enshadowed tree;
it is said that true virginity –
marker of New Right certainty,
the Free World's leaders' choice,
annihilator of AIDS, terrorist
contraceptive – is immune
to even trade union hi-jinks.
Do you believe me or do I need call
the party? A band of young conservatives
to attest the virtues of chastity?
Remember Diana, Queen of Hearts,

chaste as conspiracy, where she tamed
the coiffured lioness and spotted pard
her husband, but dashed aside
the bolts of Cupid. Lords and men
feared her popularity, and she was
Lady of the Sloane Rangers.
Remember, our sister
has never been lured by science,
she has never aspired to parliament,
to own her own business, to dress
in shapeless trousers. Growing up,
she always had girl toys
and let our boy toys be, she
bows to our inevitable muscularity.
That unpolluted temple of her mind.
It's only when girls open their legs
and let the enemy in they pollute
themselves: the soul growing putrid
and the property of her body
devalued on the blood-line market.
She is divine property and must remain so –
otherwise, her body and soul
are no better than a charnel house,
no better than dirt which is a vault for the dead,
spreading rhizomically, her abject
liquids flowing degenerate,
degraded by carnal sensuality.

SECOND BROTHER
How charming is public-school
propaganda! Not straight and dry
as lefties suppose, but musical
as Liam Gallagher.

ELDER BROTHER
Listen, I hear a cry tear the silent air.

SECOND BROTHER
I heard it too. What could it be?

ELDER BROTHER
Either someone night-stranded like ourselves
or some neighbouring forester, or, at worst,
a criminal calling to his mates.

SECOND BROTHER
Heaven keep my sister nearby:
let's take our weapons and be ready.

ELDER BROTHER
I'll call out and if he comes to us
in friendship, then great, but if not
we must be ready to defend ourselves.
God is on our side.

The Attendant Spirit dressed like a Farmhand.

I should know that cry. What are you?
Don't come too close or you'll be knifed.

Spirit
Is that the boss's son? Speak up.

Second Brother
Ah, brother, it is my father's farmhand, surely.

Elder Brother
Thyrsis? Whose magical voice
has often caused the brook to hesitate,
hold back its flow to hear his melodies,
and sweetened the sweetest flowers,
what brings you here? Has a ram or
flighty lamb or indignant wether
escaped through neglected fences?
How could you find this godforsaken place?

Spirit
My boss's eldest, and his next happiness,
I came here on more serious business
than a stray ewe, or to chase down
a thieving predator – the entire wealth of the Downs
is barely worth a thought compared
to my purpose in this twisted wood:
Where is your virgin sister?
Why isn't she here?

ELDER BROTHER
To tell the truth, farmhand,
innocently, she's lost in the land.

SPIRIT
Horrific. My fears are proven.

ELDER BROTHER
What fears, Thyrsis? Please explain.

SPIRIT
I'll tell you, it's not prurient or fabulous
(though cast as such out of ignorance)
what our muse-obsessed, *inspired* poets
tell as archetypal tales in flaming verse:
no deadly Chimeras and white-washed isles,
no atomic meltdowns that lead to hell,
for that's the case – unbelief *is* blind.
    Within the core of this hideous wood,
encased in hardwood lurks a scientist
come out of the labs of Bacchus
and Circe, some say a GM baby
himself – eminent Comus,
Nobel Laureate, deeply skilled
in his mother's arts, and here
to every thirsty wanderer,
by deception proffers
his poisonous glass,

with many conversations
mixed – a patent so lusted after
by Coca Cola – with whose sugary taste
the face turns animal, taking away
all human shape to substitute
the visage of a beast, to substitute
reason with the behaviours of that beast.
I've heard all this out tending the flocks,
watching over the interests of the estate.
At first I thought it was a pathogen
released from the government research place
that borders the wood, but no, this is a freelance
outfit operating without "controls",
though it's rumoured the government
turns a blind eye, benefits
from its "liberalities".
Each night I hear their partying.
Crazed on crystal meth
they webcam their perverse rites,
unpicking the living: torture, sadism, discovery.
They have many ways of conning
passersby into joining their experiments.
This evening after the flocks had settled
in for their rest, bellies full of grass,
I sat down upon a bank lush with ivy
and woven together with honeysuckle,
and wrapped in a pleasing melancholy,
thinking over the residues of pastoral,

singing quietly of the old ways,
I heard dance music shatter the peace,
filling the air with barbarous dissonance.
It ceased. I listened. Then silence.
Soon a soft breathing sound
rising like perfume. Silence hungered
after it. I was all ears. A soul beneath
the ribs of death? But soon I perceived
it was the voice of my honoured Lady,
your dear sister. I stood, amazed,
harrowed with grief and fear,
that poor nightingale so near
the rabble's deadly snare!
Then I plunged headlong
down the grassy paths
I know so well by day
until following my ear
I came across the spot
where that damned scientist
hid in sly disguise
(the signs I knew);
where he had already met
despite my haste,
with the innocent Lady
he wished as prey,
who had gently asked
if he'd seen two brothers
pass that way – thinking him

a worker to be trusted.
I soon guessed she meant you two,
and with that took to my heels
until I found you here.
That's all I know.

Second Brother
Oh night and shades,
joined with hell in a triple knot
against a defenceless
virgin – is this the confidence
you gave me, brother?

Elder Brother
Yes, and keep it. No science
or alchemy will open that pathway.
Virtue can't be destroyed.
It can be surprised by evil,
but not enslaved.
And even in the face
of extreme duress
she'll pass the test.
Evil will consume itself –
a putrid distillate of goodness,
sludge that won't be recycled,
or else the ozone layer will collapse
and the earth's foundations
turn to plastic in its self-consuming

rage, its maelstrom of enhancement.
Let's go now, to fight this
just war... let him be surrounded
by his Republican Guard, let him
worship his false idols, let his harpies
and hydras from all of the places
approaching peak oil surround him
with monstrous forms – I'll track
him down, and unless he
hands back our virgin wealth,
bomb him with a precision
that will take his whole family
and rabble out.

SPIRIT
Young fellow, I admire your violence,
your passion, your ideology,
but no mere bombs will bring
him down: the war is fought
with propaganda first. A mere broadcast
from his lair, a mere word leaking out,
will, as the wave of his wand,
dismember you
beyond repair.

ELDER BROTHER
Then, how did you approach near
without annihilation?

SPIRIT
A cautious approach
and deep desire
to secure your sister
reminded me of a young shearer
I knew from another country,
highly tuned to the herb he was,
and knew the names of countless
strains and species; he loved me
deeply and I loved him equally,
and I sang him songs
that brought him joy,
and in turn as the late sun
lit the fields an unanswerable red,
he handed me a bag
of small, wizened heads
he'd smuggled through customs:
the leaf was darkish
and flower-parts resinous,
it carried no seed: where I come from,
he said, my mates only smoke hydros,
and have forgotten the efficacy
of old strains grown in dirt.
It's more powerful than the stuff
praised by Cypress Hill,
more potent than a scene
from *Easy Rider* or *Cheech and Chong*.
He gave me a nod and bade me

sovran use 'gainst all enchantments,
mildew blast, or damp
or ghastly apparition. And so
I took it, though little more of it, until now,
and what he said proves true:
I knew the foul scientist
though he was disguised, and entered
the very carnality of his spells,
and survived. If you smoke a little
of this and carry some on you
(as I will give you when we go) you
may invade the dictator's palace,
where you might bravely
rush him and smash the glass
that holds the poison, and disarm
him of that weapon of mass destruction,
his wand. And though he will huff and puff,
and his rabble put on a show,
they'll soon retreat in the face
of your superior science.

ELDER BROTHER
Thyrsis. Let's do it. I have faith
in our defence shield.

> *The scene changes to a stately palace, set out with all manner of deliciousness; soft music, tables spread with all dainties. Comus appears with his crew, and the Lady sits in*

an enchanted chair, to whom he offers his vessel which she puts aside, and goes to get up.

COMUS
No, stay where you are, Lady.
Should I wave this wand
you'd turn to stone.
Your nerves colonised,
you'd be less than cyborg.

LADY
You've got my body
but not my mind.
Your science
is no heaven
for all your claims.

COMUS
What's irking you, Lady?
This is a happening place.
All smiles here. We don't let
misery through the gates.
Every pleasure you can imagine
out of your youth, anything
that takes your fancy
waits. Fresh blood
grows lively
with Cialis and Viagra.

Or a hypodermic that will make
that first breach a blast,
a rush as good as power…
Why deny yourself, why torment
those delicate limbs
for intricacy… delicacies,
clench your muscles
as if something's going to break?
You go against the call of nature,
you abominate her trust,
all good work needs its reward,
all market-places insider trading:
the law is law to those who make it:
refreshment after toil, ease after pain:
weary with being lost,
this, fair Virgin,
will pick you up!
A restoration.

LADY
It is a lie as you are a liar –
it will restore nothing
I don't already have.
What of the place
you promised, the place
you intimated was safe?
What are these aberrations,
these grotesqueries

that surround us?
Ethics protect me!
With biochemistry
and forgery you have
deceived me: vampirised
my innocence to turn me.
I will not be injected
with your liquid.
Your delicious cocktail
may satisfy a committee
of your own making,
but I'll resist: only good men
can give good things.

Comus
Good men? Don't give me
that shit. Men of the ethics
committees who give their nod
to a little more each year,
lest their institution
fall behind the scrum?
Those good men who
in their abstinence
kiss their wives
and visit brothels?
Who prescribe planetary health
and drive the thirstiest cars,
say prayers like gifts

and dodge their tax?
Why is the earth so stocked
with bounty? With enticing
smells, fruits and flocks,
oceans seething with life,
a little something
for every curious taste?
And what of the synthetics
spun from oil, and uranium
that gives the world an endless glow,
and conflict diamonds
to brighten an anniversary.
What of the mining boom
in the Antipodes, whole mountains
of ore turned to steel?
What of the naysayers
ranting on about the fate
of some weedy plant
or micro-organism? Get
perspective, Lady – we
can't be ripped off by them!
Wasted fertility,
graceful strangulation,
is not nature's wish.
If it were so, we'd
be living as slaves.
No religion could exist
as there'd be nothing to praise!

The gifts of the earth
are to be enjoyed, gorged
by its children. Let them clear
the high places of bushland
and launch their hang-gliders.
Take what's theirs, take what's ours!
We are nature's children, not her bastards.
If we left the birds to their own devices
the air would suffocate with feathers;
if we left the herds unslaughtered
they'd multiply and trample us under;
if we left the oceans untrammelled
they'd swell and break the scales,
the Deep vomiting its bile onto the land,
the swimmers come to the surface
to embrace the sun and evict
humans from their world.
Come now, Lady, stop flirting,
I know you're gagging for it:
virginity has no place on this map.
Beauty is best revealed,
unhooded it grows
with stimulation
reaching bliss,
better shared
than kept locked
within the self.
If you let time slip,

it withers like a cut rose.
Beauty is about the show,
nature's bragging rights,
to be flashed about at uptown
parties, to be flaunted
before the cameras.
Let the ugly ones stay at home:
your architecture is designed
for show. Arguing over daycare,
letting down the hems
of now too-short-skirts,
a home business
run via a slightly
out-of-date computer
just aren't you.
If you've got it, flaunt it!
Rage, rage, rage!

LADY
I hadn't planned to unlock my lips
in this desecrated air, but this charlatan
thinks he can wrap me around
his little finger, as if I'm mind-numbed.
I hate it when vice shuts virtue
down, dazzling with misinformation:
scientist, do not cite nature
as one who would have her children
waste the world's abundance

there is no agency that gives
permission for wholesale
robbery, exploitation.
Take this rare patch of bush
I have heard of in the Antipodes,
where paragliders and hang-glider pilots
destroy the last remaining flowers
of a critically endangered species
so they can leap off a mountain
into the air and fly above it all,
training their bird's-eye view,
inheritors of all they observe.
Or near at hand, the last fens
drained and the peat
smouldering with exposure,
each creature retreating then lost.
Gluttony looks the other way
as the biosphere collapses,
as birds search out trees
to nest then vanish
as their search defeats them.
Shall I go on or have I said enough?
It becomes painful to listen,
dismissed as ranting,
as inhuman soapboxing.
That's virginity, that's chastity:
intactness, but not intactness
as Monsieur Barthes would have us

read Jules Verne in his enclosed craft.
What can I say to the dancing rabble,
to the polite clergy, to the double-dealing
government minister, to the scientist
who does it all for science...
an enclosed system. My chastity
is not "goods", but of the Sun
and turns your profanity like ice.
You just don't get sublimity,
unless it's the new sublime of waste
and desecration: the teetering on the edge
of holocaust: you don't deserve
more happiness than you know.
Enjoy your consuming wit
and self-asserting rhetoric,
your pitiful dazzle of defence –
you are barely worth my contempt –
but if I tapped into grace
and turned on you, the magma
of the earth would rise up and circulate,
pillage your body's artificial magic,
wreck the structures, the monument
you've erected to self, to falseness.

Comus
She's not joking – I feel it in my bones,
she speaks with an unnatural force
in affirming nature, a cold sweat

beads my skin, fear driven deep
as thunder straight overhead
with no gap between crash
and lightning stroke,
struck down, affixed
juddering to the spot.
I must dissemble.
Try a new approach.
What! This is moralising
shit she speaks. Get a grip.
That melancholic blood of hers
is infecting me, her bleeding heart
twists anger, contra-indication…
years of research and pleasure
can't be lost: this snaps
the laws of our foundation.
Enough! One blast of this
will sweep her with bliss.
Be smart… taste…

> *The Brothers rush in with weapons ready, wrest the vessel (ampoule) out of his hand, and break it against the ground; his crew make signs of resistance, but are driven in by superior firepower; the Attendant Spirit enters.*

SPIRIT
What! Have you let the foul scientist escape?
You should have snatched his wand away

and tied him up: without his device
and its dissevering power,
we cannot free the Lady fixed
motionless with stone restraints.
But stay calm, I have another idea:
also from a shearer, but a local one
who sang the most ribald songs
ever sung – sorry, but needs must
when the Devil drives.
      There is a young straight-edge –
tattooed and wearing hemp –
not far from here, who with a swing
of her hips will sway the Severn stream,
Sabrina is her name,
gives away all that's hers to give,
though born of Locrine's
and Estrildi's adultery,
fled her crazy step-mum
and threw her sweetness
into the cross-currents of flood
to be raised up by girls of a local
coven – strong swimmers all –
and taken to Nereus's stately home –
he's one of those who's
giving his wealth away,
gone organic and communal –
who handed her to his daughters' care,
to bathe in scented oils and asphodel,

to perk her up with herbal
stimulants – *au naturel* –
till she revived and transformed
into the clear and present danger
MI5 say she is today –
goddess of the river.
She's generous: helping
feed the hungry with her
adopted father's produce,
protesting to keep the paths
open to all walkers,
helping out with addicts
driven from the streets.
Her fluids are of the healing kind.
No GM, no synthetics, nothing
killed to further life when life
is what she brings and is celebrated
by shearers and farmhands and street-people.
And as that shearer said to me,
she can unweave any synthetic
and undo the damage done by psychiatry,
if she be called upon
by song – and she will be keen
to help a virgin as once she was pursued.
I will sing her here with poetry.

SONG

Sabrina
  Hear me where you are
Fighting for fresh clear water
  In reeds the colour of your hair
Lush about the river,
  Listen for a future,
  Guardian of the last reservoir,
      Listen; recover.

Listen and appear to us
in the name of all creatures
of all oceans of all mountains
of all plains of all ravines
of all forests of all trees
of all outcrops of all valleys
of all snowfields of all glaciers
of all shorelines of all deltas
of all streams of all lakes
of all birds and beasts
that fly and run and feast
and preen and snap and dig and bite
and sing or praise the night
or day or feel the moon
in their bones or sun
themselves or who stretch across
the land or surf the waves.

In their names, on their
behalf, Sabrina, hear
our summons.
        Listen; recover.

Sabrina rises, attended by women friends, and sings.

  I hope to show
That where rushes and willow and osier grow
    We can let things be,
No need for motor boats or cars,
  Effluent pipes or phone towers,
     Fertilisers that bring algae
    To choke ducks and fish;
  I am wary of the developer's ambush,
  Building to the water's edge,
    Let the stoats hunt and squirrels forage,
  And so, farmhand, at your request
    I am here.

SPIRIT
    Sabrina dear
we beg you to use your power
to undo the bonds that skewer
this virgin to this device;
she was strapped here
by an unethical bio-engineer.

SABRINA
Farmhand, it's what I do:
no means *no*, never yes,
exquisite girl held under duress,
see me as I see you,
I will kiss your breasts,
I will fill you with zest,
I will cure you with a finger's tip,
I will kiss you on the lips,
I will coat this deathly seat
with oils that free the hands and feet,
I will diminish the spell,
I will dissolve the hard sell;
now it is time for me to go,
before morning's deadly glow.

Sabrina descends and the Lady rises out of her seat.

SPIRIT
Protester,
eco-warrior,
may your causes
outfox city ordinances,
may like-believers
expose the deceivers,
may the snowy hills
see snow and not peals
of heat mid-winter,

may the river
flow and not dry out,
may pigs snout
and grunt, not manufacture
hearts and cures
for human strife:
let each thing have its life.
Come Lady while things favour us.
let's flee this bio-party place,
lest the scientist entice
with some other pleasuring device.
Not a word until we're out
of his redoubt:
let's make our way
to your father's security,
there is a big party there tonight
where the rich and powerful will gestate
officially sanctioned schemes
to profit the kingdom:
no drugs just alcohol,
no biology outside state control,
no out of control Comus,
just good citizens looking out for us;
even the workers will put on a show
quaint dancing and singing and a row
about who won the football.
Our sudden arrival
with the stars still shining

will bring happiness to their fling.

> The scene changes, presenting town and the architect-designed house, then come in the tasteful culturally valid dancers, after them the Attendant Spirit, with the two Brothers and the Lady.

    SONG

SPIRIT
Back, workers, back, enough recreation,
Go back until you're summoned again.
There is serious art to call,
Performed by those with cultural capital,
They've all been to public school,
Where lawns and green exist still.

> This second SONG presents them to their father and mother.

>> Sir and Madam… I delight
>> in presenting a fresh delight,
>> Your offspring: the three
>>   you made as family,
>> the three who will spread
>> the family bread:
>> they have been tested
>> in disturbing ways, have braved
>> darkness and distress,
>> have kept at bay the sensuous.

The dance ends and the Spirit eulogises.

SPIRIT
So now it's time for me to fly,
to any happy climate that lies
where jungle is being peeled
away, and the locals herded
into urban penury:
though sensitive to the injury
we do to our own fair land,
don't let it be said
I am not a pragmatist:
I know to fuel our bliss
we need feed from somewhere,
be it Amazon or Congo, Nigeria
or P & G, old Borneo
or the forests of Tasmania,
to preserve here we look elsewhere.
So don't despair,
all this greenie poetry
won't mean you'll lose your luxuries.
Those of you who'd follow me,
remember the code word: LIBERTY…
virtue doesn't mean you
can't have your cake and eat it too.

    THE END

COMUS
A Mask
JOHN MILTON

A Mask

Of the Same
AUTHOR
PRESENTED
At *LUDLOW*-Castle,
1634.

THE PERSONS.

>The Attendant Spirit
>>afterwards in the habit of Thyrsis
>Comus with his crew
>The Lady
>Elder Brother
>2 Brother
>Sabrina the Nymph

The first Scene discovers a wilde Wood.

The Attendant Spirit descends or enters

Before the starry threshold of *Joves* Court
My mansion is, where those immortal shapes
Of bright aëreal Spirits live insphear'd
In Regions milde of calm and serene Ayr,
Above the smoak and stirr of this dim spot,
Which men call Earth, and with low-thoughted care
Confin'd, and pester'd in this pin-fold here,
Strive to keep up a frail, and Feaverish being
Unmindfull of the crown that Vertue gives
After this mortal change, to her true Servants
Amongst the enthron'd gods on Sainted seats.
Yet som there be that by due steps aspire
To lay their just hands on that Golden Key
That ope's the Palace of Eternity:
To such my errand is, and but for such,
I would not soil these pure Ambrosial weeds,
With the rank vapours of this Sin-worn mould.
      But to my task. *Neptune* besides the sway
Of every salt Flood, and each ebbing Stream,
Took in by lot 'twixt high, and neather *Jove*,
Imperial rule of all the Sea-girt Iles
That like to rich, and various gemms inlay
The unadorned boosom of the Deep,
Which he to grace his tributary gods

By course commits to severall goverment,
And gives them leave to wear their Saphire crowns,
And weild their little tridents, but this Ile
The greatest, and the best of all the main
He quarters to his blu-hair'd deities,
And all this tract that fronts the falling Sun
A noble Peer of mickle trust, and power
Has in his charge, with temper'd awe to guide
An old, and haughty Nation proud in Arms:
Where his fair off-spring nurs't in Princely lore,
Are coming to attend their Fathers state,
And new-entrusted Scepter, but their way
Lies through the perplex't paths of this drear Wood,
The nodding horror of whose shady brows
Threats the forlorn and wandring Passinger.
And here their tender age might suffer perill,
But that by quick command from Soveran *Jove*
I was dispatcht for their defence, and guard;
And listen why, for I will tell ye now
What never yet was heard in Tale or Song
From old, or modern Bard in Hall, or Bowr.
    Bacchus that first from out the purple Grape,
Crush't the sweet poyson of mis-used Wine
After the *Tuscan* Mariners transform'd
Coasting the *Tyrrhene* shore, as the winds listed,
On *Circes* Iland fell (who knows not *Circe*
The daughter of the Sun? Whose charmed Cup
Whoever tasted, lost his upright shape,

And downward fell into a groveling Swine)
This Nymph that gaz'd upon his clustring locks,
With Ivy berries wreath'd, and his blithe youth,
Had by him, ere he parted thence, a Son
Much like his Father, but his Mother more,
Whom therfore she brought up and *Comus* nam'd,
Who ripe, and frolick of his full grown age,
Roaving the *Celtick*, and *Iberian* fields,
At last betakes him to this ominous Wood,
And in thick shelter of black shades imbowr'd,
Excells his Mother at her mighty Art,
Offring to every weary Travailer,
His orient liquor in a Crystal Glasse,
To quench the drouth of *Phoebus*, which as they taste
(For most do taste through fond intemperate thirst)
Soon as the Potion works, their human count'nance,
Th' express resemblance of the gods, is chang'd
Into some brutish form of Woolf, or Bear,
Or Ounce, or Tiger, Hog, or bearded Goat,
All other parts remaining as they were,
And they, so perfect is their misery,
Not once perceive their foul disfigurement,
But boast themselves more comely then before
And all their friends, and native home forget
To roule with pleasure in a sensual stie.
Therfore when any favour'd of high *Jove*,
Chances to pass through this adventrous glade,
Swift as the Sparkle of a glancing Star,

I shoot from Heav'n to give him safe convoy,
As now I do: But first I must put off
These my skierobes spun out of *Iris* Wooff,
And take the Weeds and likenes of a Swain,
That to the service of this house belongs,
Who with his soft Pipe, and smooth-dittied Song,
Well knows to still the wilde winds when they roar,
And hush the waving Woods, nor of lesse faith,
And in this office of his Mountain watch,
Likeliest, and neerest to the present ayd
Of this occasion. But I hear the tread
Of hatefull steps, I must be viewles now.

> Comus *enters with a Charming Rod in one hand, his Glass in the other, with him a rout of Monsters headed like sundry sorts of wilde Beasts, but otherwise like Men and Women, their Apparel glistring, they com in making a riotous and unruly noise, with Torches in their hands.*

COMUS
The Star that bids the Shepherd fold,
Now the top of Heav'n doth hold,
And the gilded Car of Day,
His glowing Axle doth allay
In the steep *Atlantick* stream,
And the slope Sun his upward beam
Shoots against the dusky Pole,

Pacing toward the other gole
Of his Chamber in the East.
Mean while welcom Joy, and Feast,
Midnight shout, and revelry,
Tipsie dance and Jollity.
Braid your Locks with rosie Twine
Dropping odours, dropping Wine.
Rigor now is gon to bed,
And Advice with scrupulous head,
Strict Age, and sowre Severity,
With their grave Saws in slumber ly.
We that are of purer fire
Imitate the Starry Quire,
Who in their nightly watchfull Sphears,
Lead in swift round the Months and Years.
The Sounds, and Seas with all their finny drove
Now to the Moon in wavering Morrice move,
And on the Tawny Sands and Shelves,
Trip the pert Fairies and the dapper Elves;
By dimpled Brook, and Fountain brim,
The Wood-Nymphs deckt with Daisies trim,
Their merry wakes and pastimes keep:
What hath night to do with sleep?
Night hath better sweets to prove,
Venus now wakes, and wak'ns Love.
Com let us our rights begin,
Tis onely day-light that makes Sin,
Which these dun shades will ne're report.

Hail Goddesse of Nocturnal sport
Dark vaild *Cotytto*, t'whom the secret flame
Of mid-night Torches burns; mysterious Dame
That ne're art call'd, but when the Dragon woom
Of Stygian darknes spets her thickest gloom,
And makes one blot of all the ayr,
Stay thy cloudy Ebon chair,
Wherin thou rid'st with *Hecat'*, and befriend
Us thy vow'd Priests, till utmost end
Of all thy dues be done, and none left out,
Ere the blabbing Eastern scout,
The nice Morn on th'*Indian* steep
From her cabin'd loop hole peep,
And to the tel-tale Sun discry
Our conceal'd Solemnity.
Com, knit hands, and beat the ground,
In a light fantastick round.

The Measure.

Break off, break off, I feel the different pace,
Of som chast footing neer about this ground.
Run to your shrouds, within these Brakes and Trees,
Our number may affright: Som Virgin sure
(For so I can distinguish by mine Art)
Benighted in these Woods. Now to my charms,
And to my wily trains, I shall e're long
Be well stock't with as fair a herd as graz'd

About my Mother *Circe*. Thus I hurl
My dazling Spells into the spungy ayr,
Of power to cheat the eye with blear illusion,
And give it false presentments, lest the place
And my quaint habits breed astonishment,
And put the Damsel to suspicious flight,
Which must not be, for that's against my course;
I under fair pretence of friendly ends,
And well-plac't words of glozing courtesie,
Baited with reasons not unplausible
Wind me into the easie-hearted man,
And hugg him into snares. When once her eye
Hath met the vertue of this Magick dust,
I shall appear som harmles Villager
Whom thrift keeps up about his Country gear,
But here she comes, I fairly step aside
And hearken, if I may, her busines here.

   The Lady enters.

This way the noise was, if mine ear be true,
My best guide now, me thought it was the sound
Of Riot, and ill-manag'd Merriment,
Such as the jocond Flute, or gamesom Pipe
Stirs up among the loose unleter'd Hinds,
When for their teeming Flocks, and granges full
In wanton dance they praise the bounteous Pan,
And thank the gods amiss. I should be loath

To meet the rudeness, and swill'd insolence
Of such late Wassailers; yet O where els
Shall I inform my unacquainted feet
In the blind mazes of this tangl'd Wood?
My Brothers when they saw me wearied out
With this long way, resolving here to lodge
Under the spreading favour of these Pines,
Stept as they se'd to the next Thicket side
To bring me Berries, or such cooling fruit
As the kind hospitable Woods provide.
They left me then, when the gray-hooded Eev'n
Like a sad Votarist in Palmers weed
Rose from the hindmost wheels of *Phoebus* wain.
But where they are, and why they came not back,
Is now the labour of my thoughts; 'tis likeliest
They had ingag'd their wandring steps too far,
And envious darknes, e're they could return,
Had stole them from me, els O theevish Night
Why shouldst thou, but for som fellonious end,
In thy dark lantern thus close up the Stars,
That nature hung in Heav'n, and fill'd their Lamps
With everlasting oil, to give due light
To the misled and lonely Travailer?
This is the place, as well as I may guess,
Whence eev'n now the tumult of loud Mirth
Was rife, and perfet in my list'ning ear,
Yet nought but single darknes do I find.
What might this be? A thousand fantasies

Begin to throng into my memory
Of calling shapes and beckning shadows dire,
And airy tongues, that syllable mens names
On Sands, and Shoars, and desert Wildernesses.
These thoughts may startle well, but not astound
The vertuous mind, that ever walks attended
By a strong siding champion Conscience. —
O welcom pure ey'd Faith, white-handed Hope,
Thou hov'ring Angel girt with golden wings,
And thou unblemish't form of Chastity,
I see ye visibly, and now beleeve
That he, the Supreme good, t'whom all things ill
Are but as slavish officers of vengeance,
Would send a glistring Guardian if need were
To keep my life and honour unassail'd.
Was I deceiv'd, or did a sable cloud
Turn forth her silver lining on the night?
I did not err, there does a sable cloud
Turn forth her silver lining on the night,
And casts a gleam over this tufted Grove.
I cannot hallow to my Brothers, but
Such noise as I can make to be heard farthest
Ile venter, for my new enliv'nd spirits
Prompt me; and they perhaps are not far off.

SONG

Sweet Echo, sweetest Nymph that liv'st unseen
  Within thy airy shell
  By slow Meander's *margent green,*
And in the violet imbroider'd vale
  Where the love-lorn Nightingale
Nightly to thee her sad Song mourneth well.
  Canst thou not tell me of a gentle Pair
    That likest thy Narcissus *are?*
      O if thou have
    Hid them in some flowry Cave,
      Tell me but where
Sweet Queen of Parly, Daughter of the Sphear,
  So maist thou be translated to the skies,
And give resounding grace to all Heav'ns Harmonies.

COMUS
Can any mortal mixture of Earths mould
Breath such Divine inchanting ravishment?
Sure somthing holy lodges in that brest,
And with these raptures moves the vocal air
To testifie his hidd'n residence;
How sweetly did they float upon the wings
Of silence, through the empty-vaulted night
At every fall smoothing the Raven doune
Of darknes till it smil'd: I have oft heard
My mother *Circe* with the Sirens three,

Amid'st the flowry-kirtl'd *Naiades*
Culling their Potent hearbs, and balefull drugs,
Who as they sung, would take the prison'd soul,
And lap it in *Elysium, Scylla* wept,
And chid her barking waves into attention,
And fell *Charybdis* murmur'd soft applause:
Yet they in pleasing slumber lull'd the sense,
And in sweet madnes rob'd it of it self,
But such a sacred, and home-felt delight,
Such sober certainty of waking bliss
I never heard till now. Ile speak to her
And she shall be my Queen. Hail forren wonder
Whom certain these rough shades did never breed
Unlesse the Goddes that in rurall shrine
Dwell'st here with *Pan*, or *Silvan*, by blest Song
Forbidding every bleak unkindly Fog
To touch the prosperous growth of this tall Wood.

Lady
Nay gentle Shepherd ill is lost that praise
That is addrest to unattending Ears,
Not any boast of skill, but extreme shift
How to regain my sever'd company
Compell'd me to awake the courteous Echo
To give me answer from her mossie Couch.

Comus
What chance good Lady hath bereft you thus?

Lady
Dim darknes, and this leavy Labyrinth.

Comus
Could that divide you from neer-ushering guides?

Lady
They left me weary on a grassie terf.

Comus
By falshood, or discourtesie, or why?

Lady
To seek i'th vally som cool friendly Spring.

Comus
And left your fair side all unguarded Lady?

Lady
They were but twain, and purpos'd quick return.

Comus
Perhaps fore-stalling night prevented them.

Lady
How easie my misfortune is to hit!

Comus
Imports their loss, beside the present need?

Lady
No less then if I should my brothers loose.

Comus
Were they of manly prime, or youthful bloom?

Lady
As smooth as *Hebe*'s their unrazor'd lips.

Comus
Two such I saw, what time the labour'd Oxe
In his loose traces from the furrow came,
And the swink't hedger, at his Supper sate;
I saw them under a green mantling vine
That crawls along the side of yon small hill,
Plucking ripe clusters from the tender shoots,
Their port was more then human, as they stood;
I took it for a faëry vision
Of som gay creatures of the element
That in the colours of the Rainbow live
And play i'th plighted clouds. I was aw-strook,
And as I past, I worshipt: if those you seek,
It were a journey like the path to Heav'n
To help you find them.

LADY
Gentle villager
What readiest way would bring me to that place?

COMUS
Due west it rises from this shrubby point.

LADY
To find out that, good Shepherd, I suppose,
In such a scant allowance of Star-light,
Would overtask the best Land-Pilots art,
Without the sure guess of well-practiz'd feet.

COMUS
I know each lane, and every alley green
Dingle, or bushy dell of this wilde Wood,
And every bosky bourn from side to side
My daily walks and ancient neighbourhood,
And if your stray attendance be yet lodg'd,
Or shroud within these limits, I shall know
Ere morrow wake, or the low roosted lark
From her thach't pallat rowse, if otherwise
I can conduct you Lady to a low
But loyal cottage, where you may be safe
Till further quest'.

LADY
Shepherd I take thy word,

And trust thy honest offer'd courtesie,
Which oft is sooner found in lowly sheds
With smoaky rafters, then in tapstry Halls
And Courts of Princes, where it first was nam'd,
And yet is most pretended: In a place
Less warranted then this, or less secure
I cannot be, that I should fear to change it,
Eie me blest Providence, and square my triall
To my proportion'd strength. Shepherd lead on.

The two Brothers.

ELDER BROTHER
Unmuffle ye faint stars, and thou fair Moon
That wontst to love the travailer's benizon,
Stoop thy pale visage through an amber cloud,
And disinherit *Chaos*, that raigns here
In double night of darknes, and of shades;
Or if your influence be quite damm'd up
With black usurping mists, som gentle taper
Though a rush Candle from the wicker hole
Of som clay habitation visit us
With thy long levell'd rule of streaming light,
And thou shalt be our star of *Arcady*,
Or *Tyrian* Cynosure.

2 BROTHER
Or if our eyes

Be barr'd that happines, might we but hear
The folded flocks pen'd in their watled cotes,
Or sound of pastoral reed with oaten stops,
Or whistle from the Lodge, or village cock
Count the night watches to his feathery Dames,
T'would be som solace yet, som little chearing
In this close dungeon of innumerous bowes.
But O that haples virgin our lost sister
Where may she wander now, whether betake her
From the chill dew, amongst rude burrs and thistles?
Perhaps som cold bank is her boulster now
Or 'gainst the rugged bark of som broad Elm
Leans her unpillow'd head fraught with sad fears.
What if in wild amazement, and affright,
Or while we speak within the direfull grasp
Of Savage hunger, or of Savage heat?

ELDER BROTHER
Peace brother, be not over-exquisite
To cast the fashion of uncertain evils;
For grant they be so, while they rest unknown,
What need a man forestall his date of grief,
And run to meet what he would most avoid?
Or if they be but false alarms of Fear,
How bitter is such self-delusion?
I do not think my sister so to seek,
Or so unprincipl'd in vertues book,
And the sweet peace that goodnes boosoms ever,

As that the single want of light and noise
(Not being in danger, as I trust she is not)
Could stir the constant mood of her calm thoughts,
And put them into mis-becoming plight.
Vertue could see to do what vertue would
By her own radiant light, though Sun and Moon
Were in the flat Sea sunk. And Wisdoms self
Oft seeks to sweet retired Solitude,
Where with her best nurse Contemplation
She plumes her feathers, and lets grow her wings
That in the various bussle of resort
Were all to ruffl'd, and somtimes impair'd.
He that has light within his own cleer brest
May sit i'th center, and enjoy bright day,
But he that hides a dark soul, and foul thoughts
Benighted walks under the mid-day Sun;
Himself is his own dungeon.

2 Brother
Tis most true
That musing meditation most affects
The Pensive secrecy of desert cell,
Far from the cheerfull haunt of men, and herds,
And sits as safe as in a Senat house,
For who would rob a Hermit of his Weeds,
His few Books, or his Beads, or Maple Dish,
Or do his gray hairs any violence?
But beauty like the fair Hesperian Tree

Laden with blooming gold, had need the guard
Of dragon watch with uninchanted eye,
To save her blossoms, and defend her fruit
From the rash hand of bold Incontinence.
You may as well spred out the unsun'd heaps
Of Misers treasure by an out-laws den,
And tell me it is safe, as bid me hope
Danger will wink on Opportunity,
And let a single helpless maiden pass
Uninjur'd in this wilde surrounding wast.
Of night, or lonelines it recks me not,
I fear the dred events that dog them both,
Lest som ill greeting touch attempt the person
Of our unowned sister.

Elder Brother
I do not, brother,
Inferr, as if I thought my sisters state
Secure without all doubt, or controversie:
Yet where an equall poise of hope and fear
Does arbitrate th'event, my nature is
That I encline to hope, rather then fear,
And gladly banish squint suspicion.
My sister is not so defenceless left
As you imagine, she has a hidden strength
Which you remember not.

2 Brother
What hidden strength,
Unless the strength of Heav'n, if you mean that?

Elder Brother
I mean that too, but yet a hidden strength
Which if Heav'n gave it, may be term'd her own:
'Tis chastity, my brother, chastity:
She that has that, is clad in compleat steel,
And like a quiver'd Nymph with Arrows keen
May trace huge Forests, and unharbour'd Heaths,
Infamous Hills, and sandy perilous wildes,
Where through the sacred rayes of Chastity,
No savage fierce, Bandite, or mountaneer
Will dare to soyl her Virgin purity,
Yea there, where very desolation dwels
By grots, and caverns shag'd with horrid shades,
She may pass on with unblench't majesty,
Be it not don in pride, or in presumption.
Som say no evil thing that walks by night
In fog, or fire, by lake, or moorish fen,
Blew meager Hag, or stubborn unlaid ghost,
That breaks his magick chains at *curfeu* time,
No goblin or swart Faëry of the mine,
Hath hurtfull power o're true virginity.
Do ye beleeve me yet, or shall I call
Antiquity from the old Schools of Greece
To testifie the arms of Chastity?

Hence had the huntress *Dian* her dred bow,
Fair silver-shafted Queen for ever chaste,
Wherwith she tam'd the brinded lioness
And spotted mountain pard, but set at nought
The frivolous bolt of *Cupid*, gods and men
Fear'd her stern frown, and she was queen oth' Woods.
What was that snaky-headed *Gorgon* sheild
That wise *Minerva* wore, unconquer'd Virgin,
Wherwith she freez'd her foes to congeal'd stone?
But rigid looks of Chast austerity
And noble grace that dash't brute violence
With sudden adoration, and blank aw.
So dear to Heav'n is Saintly chastity,
That when a soul is found sincerely so,
A thousand liveried Angels lacky her,
Driving far off each thing of sin and guilt,
And in cleer dream, and solemn vision
Tell her of things that no gross ear can hear,
Till oft convers with heav'nly habitants
Begin to cast a beam on th' outward shape,
The unpolluted temple of the mind,
And turns it by degrees to the souls essence,
Till all be made immortal: but when lust
By unchaste looks, loose gestures, and foul talk,
But most by leud and lavish act of sin,
Lets in defilement to the inward parts,
The soul grows clotted by contagion,
Imbodies, and imbrutes, till she quite loose

The divine property of her first being.
Such are those thick and gloomy shadows damp
Oft seen in Charnell vaults, and Sepulchers
Lingering, and sitting by a new made grave,
As loath to leave the body that it lov'd,
And link't it self by carnal sensualty
To a degenerate and degraded state.

2 BROTHER
How charming is divine Philosophy!
Not harsh, and crabbed as dull fools suppose,
But musical as is *Apollo*'s lute,
And a perpetual feast of nectar'd sweets,
Where no crude surfet raigns.

ELDER BROTHER
List, list, I hear
Som far off hallow break the silent Air.

2 BROTHER
Methought so too; what should it be?

ELDER BROTHER
For certain
Either som one like us night-founder'd here,
Or els som neighbour Wood-man, or at worst,
Som roaving Robber calling to his fellows.

2 Brother
Heav'n keep my sister, agen agen and near,
Best draw, and stand upon our guard.

Elder Brother
Ile hallow,
If he be friendly he comes well, if not,
Defence is a good cause, and Heav'n be for us.

The Attendant Spirit habited like a Shepherd.

That hallow I should know, what are you? speak;
Com not too neer, you fall on iron stakes else.

Spirit
What voice is that, my young Lord? speak agen.

2 Brother
O brother, 'tis my father Shepherd sure.

Elder Brother
Thyrsis? Whose artful strains have oft delaid
The huddling brook to hear his madrigal,
And sweeten'd every muskrose of the dale,
How cam'st thou here good Swain? hath any ram
Slip't from the fold, or young Kid lost his dam,
Or straggling weather the pen't flock forsook?
How couldst thou find this dark sequester'd nook?

SPIRIT
O my lov'd masters heir, and his next joy,
I came not here on such a trivial toy
As a stray'd Ewe, or to pursue the stealth
Of pilfering Woolf, not all the fleecy wealth
That doth enrich these Downs, is worth a thought
To this my errand, and the care it brought.
But O my Virgin Lady, where is she?
How chance she is not in your company?

ELDER BROTHER
To tell thee sadly Shepherd, without blame,
Or our neglect, we lost her as we came.

SPIRIT
Ay me unhappy then my fears are true.

ELDER BROTHER
What fears good *Thyrsis*? Prethee briefly shew.

SPIRIT
Ile tell ye, 'tis not vain, or fabulous,
(Though so esteem'd by shallow ignorance)
What the sage Poëts taught by th'heav'nly Muse,
Storied of old in high immortal vers
Of dire *Chimera*'s and inchanted Iles,
And rifted Rocks whose entrance leads to hell,
For such there be, but unbelief is blind.

Within the navil of this hideous Wood,
Immur'd in cypress shades a Sorcerer dwels
Of *Bacchus*, and of *Circe* born, great *Comus*,
Deep skill'd in all his mothers witcheries,
And here to every thirsty wanderer,
By sly enticement gives his banefull cup,
With many murmurs mixt, whose pleasing poison
The visage quite transforms of him that drinks,
And the inglorious likenes of a beast
Fixes instead, unmoulding reasons mintage
Character'd in the face; this have I learn't
Tending my flocks hard by i'th hilly crofts,
That brow this bottom glade, whence night by night
He and his monstrous rout are heard to howl
Like stabl'd wolves, or tigers at their prey,
Doing abhorred rites to *Hecate*
In their obscured haunts of inmost bowres.
Yet have they many baits, and guileful spells
To inveigle and invite th' unwary sense
Of them that pass unweeting by the way.
This evening late by then the chewing flocks
Had ta'n their supper on the savoury Herb
Of Knot-grass dew-besprent, and were in fold,
I sate me down to watch upon a bank
With Ivy canopied, and interwove
With flaunting Hony-suckle, and began
Wrapt in a pleasing fit of melancholy
To meditate my rural minstrelsie,

Till fancy had her fill, but ere a close
The wonted roar was up amidst the Woods,
And fill'd the Air with barbarous dissonance,
At which I ceas't, and listen'd them a while,
Till an unusual stop of sudden silence
Gave respite to the drowsie frighted steeds
That draw the litter of close-curtain'd sleep.
At last a soft and solemn breathing sound
Rose like a steam of rich distill'd Perfumes,
And stole upon the Air, that even Silence
Was took e're she was ware, and wish't she might
Deny her nature, and be never more
Still to be so displac't. I was all eare,
And took in strains that might create a soul
Under the ribs of Death; but O ere long
Too well I did perceive it was the voice
Of my most honour'd Lady, your dear sister.
Amaz'd I stood, harrow'd with grief and fear,
And O poor hapless Nightingale thought I,
How sweet thou sing'st, how neer the deadly snare!
Then down the Lawns I ran with headlong hast
Through paths, and turnings oft'n trod by day,
Till guided by mine ear I found the place
Where that damn'd wisard hid in sly disguise
(For so by certain signes I knew) had met
Already, ere my best speed could prævent,
The aidless innocent Lady his wish't prey,
Who gently ask't if he had seen such two,

Supposing him som neighbour villager;
Longer I durst not stay, but soon I guess't
Ye were the two she mean't, with that I sprung
Into swift flight, till I had found you here,
But furder know I not.

2 BROTHER
O night and shades,
How are ye joyn'd with hell in triple knot
Against th'unarmed weakness of one Virgin
Alone, and helpless! Is this the confidence
You gave me Brother'

ELDER BROTHER
Yes, and keep it still,
Lean on it safely, not a period
Shall be unsaid for me: against the threats
Of malice or of sorcery, or that power
Which erring men call Chance, this I hold firm;
Vertue may be assail'd, but never hurt,
Surpriz'd by unjust force, but not enthrall'd,
Yea even that which mischief meant most harm,
Shall in the happy trial prove most glory.
But evil on it self shall back recoyl,
And mix no more with goodness, when at last
Gather'd like scum, and setl'd to it self
It shall be in eternal restless change
Self-fed, and self-consum'd; if this fail,

The pillar'd firmament is rott'nness,
And earths base built on stubble. But com let's on.
Against th' opposing will and arm of Heav'n
May never this just sword be lifted up,
But for that damn'd magician, let him be girt
With all the greisly legions that troop
Under the sooty flag of *Acheron*,
Harpyies and *Hydras*, or all the monstrous forms;
'Twixt *Africa*, and *Inde*, Ile find him out,
And force him to restore his purchase back,
Or drag him by the curls, to a foul death,
Curs'd as his life.

SPIRIT
Alas good ventrous youth,
I love thy courage yet and bold Emprise,
But here thy sword can do thee little stead;
Farr other arms, and other weapons must
Be those that quell the might of hellish charms,
He with his bare wand can unthred thy joynts,
And crumble all thy sinews.

ELDER BROTHER
Why, prethee Shepherd
How durst thou then thy self approach so neer
As to make this relation?

Spirit
Care and utmost shifts
How to secure the Lady from surprisal,
Brought to my mind a certain Shepherd Lad
Of small regard to see to, yet well skill'd
In every vertuous plant and healing herb
That spreads her verdant leaf to th'morning ray,
He lov'd me well, and oft would beg me sing,
Which when I did, he on the tender grass
Would sit, and hearken even to ecstasie,
And in requitall ope his leather'n scrip,
And shew me simples of a thousand names
Telling their strange and vigorous faculties;
Amongst the rest a small unsightly root,
But of divine effect, he cull'd me out;
The leaf was darkish, and had prickles on it,
But in another Countrey, as he said,
Bore a bright golden flowre, but not in this soyl:
Unknown, and like esteem'd, and the dull swayn
Treads on it daily with his clouted shoon,
And yet more med'cinal is it then that *Moly*
That *Hermes* once to wise *Ulysses* gave;
He call'd it *Hæmony*, and gave it me,
And bade me keep it as of sovran use
'Gainst all inchantments, mildew blast, or damp
Or gastly furies apparition;
I purs't it up, but little reck'ning made,
Till now that this extremity compell'd,

But now I find it true; for by this means
I knew the foul inchanter though disguis'd,
Enter'd the very lime-twigs of his spells,
And yet came off: if you have this about you
(As I will give you when we go) you may
Boldly assault the necromancers hall;
Where if he be, with dauntless hardihood,
And brandish't blade rush on him, break his glass,
And shed the lushious liquor on the ground,
But sease his wand; though he and his curst crew
Feirce signe of battail make, and menace high,
Or like the sons of *Vulcan* vomit smoak,
Yet will they soon retire, if he but shrink.

ELDER BROTHER
Thyrsis lead on apace, Ile follow thee,
And som good angel bear a sheild before us.

> *The Scene changes to a stately Palace, set out with all manner of deliciousness; soft Musick, Tables spred with all dainties.* Comus *appears with his rabble, and the Lady set in an inchanted Chair, to whom he offers his Glass, which she puts by, and goes about to rise.*

COMUS
Nay Lady sit; if I but wave this wand,
Your nervs are all chain'd up in Alablaster,

And you a statue; or as *Daphne* was
Root-bound, that fled *Apollo*,

Lady
Fool do not boast,
Thou canst not touch the freedom of my minde
With all thy charms, although this corporal rinde
Thou haste immanacl'd, while Heav'n sees good.

Comus
Why are you vext Lady? why do you frown?
Here dwell no frowns, nor anger, from these gates
Sorrow flies farr: See here be all the pleasures
That fancy can beget on youthfull thoughts,
When the fresh blood grows lively, and returns
Brisk as the *April* buds in Primrose-season.
And first behold this cordial Julep here
That flames, and dances in his crystal bounds
With spirits of balm, and fragrant Syrops mixt.
Not that *Nepenthes* which the wife of *Thone*,
In *Egypt* gave to *Jove*-born *Helena*
Is of such power to stir up joy as this,
To life so friendly, or so cool to thirst.
Why should you be so cruel to your self,
And to those dainty limms which nature lent
For gentle usage, and soft delicacy?
But you invert the cov'nants of her trust,
And harshly deal like an ill borrower

With that which you receiv'd on other terms,
Scorning the unexempt condition
By which all mortal frailty must subsist,
Refreshment after toil, ease after pain,
That have been tir'd all day without repast,
And timely rest have wanted, but fair Virgin
This will restore all soon.

LADY
'Twill not false traitor,
'Twill not restore the truth and honesty
That thou hast banish't from thy tongue with lies,
Was this the cottage, and the safe abode
Thou told'st me of? What grim aspects are these,
These oughly-headed Monsters? Mercy guard me!
Hence with thy brew'd inchantments, foul deceiver,
Hast thou betrai'd my credulous innocence
With visor'd falsehood, and base forgery,
And wouldst thou seek again to trap me here
With lickerish baits fit to ensnare a brute?
Were it a draft for *Juno* when she banquets,
I would not taste thy treasonous offer; none
But such as are good men can give good things,
And that which is not good, is not delicious
To a wel-govern'd and wise appetite.

COMUS
O foolishnes of men! that lend their ears

To those budge doctors of the *Stoick* Furr,
And fetch their precepts from the *Cynick* Tub,
Praising the lean and sallow Abstinence.
Wherefore did Nature powre her bounties forth,
With such a full and unwithdrawing hand,
Covering the earth with odours, fruits, and flocks,
Thronging the Seas with spawn innumerable,
But all to please, and sate the curious taste?
And set to work millions of spinning Worms,
That in their green shops weave the smooth-hair'd silk
To deck her Sons; and that no corner might
Be vacant of her plenty, in her own loyns
She hutch't th'all-worshipt ore, and precious gems
To store her children with; if all the world
Should in a pet of temperance feed on Pulse,
Drink the clear stream, and nothing wear but Frieze,
Th'all-giver would be unthank't, would be unprais'd,
Not half his riches known, and yet despis'd,
And we should serve him as a grudging master,
As a penurious niggard of his wealth,
And live like Natures bastards, not her sons,
Who would be quite surcharg'd with her own weight,
And strangl'd with her waste fertility;
Th'earth cumber'd, and the wing'd air dark't with plumes,
The herds would over-multitude their Lords,
The Sea o'refraught would swell, & th'unsought diamonds
Would so emblaze the forhead of the Deep,
And so bestudd with Stars, that they below

Would grow inur'd to light, and com at last
To gaze upon the Sun with shameless brows.
List Lady be not coy, and be not cosen'd
With that same vaunted name Virginity,
Beauty is nature's coyn, must not be hoorded,
But must be currant, and the good thereof
Consists in mutual and partak'n bliss,
Unsavoury in th'injoyment of it self.
If you let slip time, like a neglected rose
It withers on the stalk with languish't head.
Beauty is natures brag, and must be shown
In courts, at feasts, and high solemnities
Where most may wonder at the workmanship;
It is for homely features to keep home,
They had their name thence; course complexions
And cheeks of sorry grain will serve to ply
The sampler, and to teize the huswifes wooll.
What need a vermeil-tinctur'd lip for that
Love-darting eyes, or tresses like the Morn?
There was another meaning in these gifts,
Think what, and be adviz'd, you are but young yet.

LADY
I had not thought to have unlockt my lips
In this unhallow'd air, but that this Jugler
Would think to charm my judgement, as mine eyes,
Obtruding false rules pranckt in reasons garb.
I hate when vice can bolt her arguments,

And vertue has no tongue to check her pride:
Impostor do not charge most innocent nature,
As if she would her children should be riotous
With her abundance, she good cateress
Means her provision onely to the good
That live according to her sober laws,
And holy dictate of spare Temperance:
If every just man that now pines with want
Had but a moderate and beseeming share
Of that which lewdly-pamper'd Luxury
Now heaps upon som few with vast excess,
Natures full blessings would be well dispenc't
In unsuperfluous eeven proportion,
And she no whit encomber'd with her store,
And then the giver would be better thank't,
His praise due paid, for swinish gluttony
Ne're looks to Heav'n amidst his gorgeous feast,
But with besotted base ingratitude
Cramms, and blasphemes his feeder. Shall I go on?
Or have I said anough? To him that dares
Arm his profane tongue with contemptuous words
Against the Sun-clad power of Chastity,
Fain would I somthing say, yet to what end?
Thou hast nor Eare, nor Soul to apprehend
The sublime notion, and high mystery
That must be utter'd to unfold the sage
And serious doctrine of Virginity,
And thou art worthy that thou shouldst not know

More happines then this thy present lot.
Enjoy your deer Wit, and gay Rhetorick
That hath so well been taught her dazling fence,
Thou art not fit to hear thy self convinc't;
Yet should I try, the uncontrouled worth
Of this pure cause would kindle my rap't spirits
To such a flame of sacred vehemence,
That dumb things would be mov'd to sympathize,
And the brute Earth would lend her nerves, and shake,
Till all thy magick structures rear'd so high,
Were shatter'd into heaps o're thy false head.

COMUS
She fables not, I feel that I do fear
Her words set off by som superior power;
And though not mortal, yet a cold shuddring dew
Dips me all o're, as when the wrath of *Jove*
Speaks thunder, and the chains of *Erebus*
To som of *Saturns* crew. I must dissemble,
And try her yet more strongly. Com, no more,
This is meer moral babble, and direct
Against the canon laws of our foundation;
I must not suffer this, yet 'tis but the lees
And setlings of a melancholy blood;
But this will cure all streight, one sip of this
Will bathe the drooping spirits in delight
Beyond the bliss of dreams. Be wise, and taste.

The Brothers rush in with Swords drawn, wrest his Glass out of his hand, and break it against the ground; his rout make signe of resistance, but are all driven in; The Attendant Spirit comes in.

SPIRIT
What, have you let the false enchanter scape?
O ye mistook, ye should have snatcht his wand
And bound him fast; without his rod revers't,
And backward mutters of dissevering power,
We cannot free the Lady that sits here
In stony fetters fixt, and motionless;
Yet stay, be not disturb'd, now I bethink me,
Som other means I have which may be us'd,
Which once of *Meliboeus* old I learnt
The soothest Shepherd that ere pip't on plains.
There is a gentle Nymph not farr from hence,
That with moist curb sways the smooth Severn stream,
Sabrina is her name, a Virgin pure,
Whilom she was the daughter of *Locrine*,
That had the Scepter from his father *Brute*.
The guiltless damsell flying the mad pursuit
Of her enraged stepdam *Guendolen*,
Commended her fair innocence to the flood
That stay'd her flight with his cross-flowing course,
The water Nymphs that in the bottom plaid,
Held up their pearled wrists and took her in,
Bearing her straight to aged *Nereus* Hall,

Who piteous of her woes, rear'd her lank head,
And gave her to his daughters to imbathe
In nectar'd lavers strew'd with Asphodil,
And through the porch and inlet of each sense
Dropt in Ambrosial Oils till she reviv'd,
And underwent a quick immortal change
Made Goddess of the River; still she retains
Her maid'n gentlenes, and oft at Eeve
Visits the herds along the twilight meadows,
Helping all urchin blasts, and ill luck signes
That the shrewd medling Elf delights to make,
Which she with pretious viol'd liquors heals.
For which the Shepherds at their festivals
Carrol her goodnes loud in rustick layes,
And throw sweet garland wreaths into her stream
Of pancies, pinks, and gaudy Daffadils.
And, as the old Swain said, she can unlock
The clasping charm, and thaw the numming spell,
If she be right invok't in warbled Song,
For maid'nhood she loves, and will be swift
To aid a Virgin, such as was her self
In hard besetting need, this will I try
And adde the power of som adjuring verse.

SONG

Sabrina fair
  Listen where thou art sitting
Under the glassie, cool, translucent wave,
  In twisted braids of Lillies knitting
The loose train of thy amber-dropping hair,
  Listen for dear honours sake,
  Goddess of the silver lake,
      Listen and save.

Listen and appear to us
In name of great *Oceanus*,
By the earth-shaking *Neptune*'s mace,
And *Tethys* grave majestick pace,
By hoary *Nereus* wrincled look,
And the *Carpathian* wisards hook,
By scaly *Tritons* winding shell,
And old sooth-saying *Glaucus* spell,
By *Leucothea*'s lovely hands,
And her son that rules the strands,
By *Thetis* tinsel-slipper'd feet,
And the Songs of *Sirens* sweet,
By dead *Parthenope*'s dear tomb,
And fair *Ligea*'s golden comb,
Wherwith she sits on diamond rocks
Sleeking her soft alluring locks,
By all the *Nymphs* that nightly dance

Upon thy streams with wily glance,
Rise, rise, and heave thy rosie head
From thy coral-pav'n bed,
And bridle in thy headlong wave,
Till thou our summons answer'd have.
Listen and save.

>   *Sabrina rises, attended by water-Nymphs, and sings.*

  By the rushy-fringed bank,
Where grows the Willow and the Osier dank,
    My sliding Chariot stayes,
Thick set with Agat, and the azurn sheen
    Of Turkis blew, and Emrauld green
        That in the channell strayes,
      Whilst from off the waters fleet
      Thus I set my printless feet
      O're the Cowslips Velvet head,
        That bends not as I tread,
      Gentle swain at thy request
        I am here.

SPIRIT
Goddess dear
We implore thy powerful hand
To undoe the charmed band
Of true Virgin here distrest,
Through the force, and through the wile

Of unblest inchanter vile.

SABRINA
Shepherd 'tis my office best
To help insnared chastity;
Brightest Lady look on me,
Thus I sprinkle on thy brest
Drops that from my fountain pure,
I have kept of pretious cure,
Thrice upon thy fingers tip,
Thrice upon thy rubied lip,
Next this marble venom'd seat
Smear'd with gumms of glutenous heat
I touch with chaste palms moist and cold,
Now the spell hath lost his hold;
And I must haste ere morning hour
To wait in *Amphitrite*'s bowr.

Sabrina descends, and the Lady rises out of her seat.

SPIRIT
Virgin, daughter of *Locrine*
Sprung of old *Anchises* line,
May thy brimmed waves for this
Their full tribute never miss
From a thousand petty rills,
That tumble down the snowy hills:
Summer drouth, or singed air

Never scorch thy tresses fair,
Nor wet *Octobers* torrent flood
Thy molten crystal fill with mudd;
May thy billows rowl ashoar
The beryl, and the golden ore,
May thy lofty head be crown'd
With many a tower and terrass round,
And here and there thy banks upon
With Groves of myrrhe, and cinnamon.
Com Lady while Heaven lends us grace,
Let us fly this cursed place,
Lest the Sorcerer us intice
With som other new device.
Not a waste, or needless sound
Till we com to holier ground,
I shall be your faithfull guide
Through this gloomy covert wide,
And not many furlongs thence
Is your Fathers residence,
Where this night are met in state
Many a friend to gratulate
His wish't presence, and beside
All the Swains that there abide,
With Jiggs, and rural dance resort,
We shall catch them at their sport,
And our sudden coming there
Will double all their mirth and chere;
Com let us haste, the Stars grow high,

But night sits monarch yet in the mid sky.

> *The Scene changes presenting* Ludlow *Town and the Presidents Castle, then com in Countrey-Dancers, after them the Attendant Spirit, with the two Brothers and the Lady.*

SONG

    Spirit
Back Shepherds, back, anough your play,
Till next Sun-shine holiday,
Here be without duck or nod
Other trippings to be trod
Of lighter toes, and such Court guise
As Mercury did first devise
With the mincing Dryades
On the Lawns, and on the Leas.

> *This second SONG presents them to their father and mother.*

Noble Lord, and Lady bright,
I have brought ye new delight,
Here behold so goodly grown
  Three fair branches of your own,
Heav'n hath timely tri'd their youth,
Their faith, their patience, and their truth,

And sent them here through hard assays
With a crown of deathless Praise,
To triumph in victorious dance
O're sensual Folly, and Intemperance.

The dances ended, the Spirit Epiloguizes.

SPIRIT
To the Ocean now I fly,
And those happy climes that ly
Where day never shuts his eye,
Up in the broad fields of the sky:
There I suck the liquid ayr
All amidst the Gardens fair
Of *Hesperus*, and his daughters three
That sing about the golden tree:
Along the crisped shades and bowres
Revels the spruce and jocond Spring,
The Graces, and the rosie-boosom'd Howres,
Thither all their bounties bring,
That there eternal Summer dwels,
And West winds, with musky wing
About the cedar'n alleys fling
Nard, and *Cassia*'s balmy smels.
Iris there with humid bow,
Waters the odorous banks that blow
Flowers of more mingled hew
Then her purfl'd scarf can shew,

And drenches with *Elysian* dew
(List mortals, if your ears be true)
Beds of *Hyacinth*, and roses
Where young Adonis oft reposes,
Waxing well of his deep wound
In slumber soft, and on the ground
Sadly sits th'*Assyrian* Queen;
But far above in spangled sheen
Celestial *Cupid* her fam'd son advanc't,
Holds his dear *Psyche* sweet intranc't
After her wandring labours long,
Till free consent the gods among
Make her his eternal Bride,
And from her fair unspotted side
Two blissful twins are to be born,
Youth and Joy; so *Jove* hath sworn.
    But now my task is smoothly don,
I can fly, or I can run
Quickly to the green earths end,
Where the bow'd welkin slow doth bend,
And from thence can soar as soon
To the corners of the Moon.
    Mortals that would follow me,
Love vertue, she alone is free,
She can teach ye how to clime
Higher then the Spheary chime;
Or if Vertue feeble were,
Heav'n it self would stoop to her.

    THE END

My *Comus*, Milton's *Comus:* an afterword
John Kinsella

My *Comus* is an environmentalist dialogic poem. I hope I have operated in the spirit of Milton's original *Comus*. I have certainly used it as a literal template, intertexting and dialoguing with the original. If the tone lends itself to irony, it's not at the expense of Milton's work, which I see as an environmentalist work in the first place. However, my *Comus* is also one tormented by its own celebration – the tension is in the need for constraint, a fear that the darkness of humanity will overwhelm the telling of the tale. Maybe Milton's is that as well – one could certainly argue this. Comus, the character, the figure, is a darker character than many observe. Comus is the evil in all of us. My Comus is a genetic scientist – I perceive the altering of genes as a basic wrong against the state of nature – and I am one who believes in mutual aid and not natural selection! But I've met some extremely decent genetic scientists, whose deep conviction is that they are doing something for the betterment of humanity.

And that's the rub. So, is it about the vilification of those some of us consider to be acting against the best interests of the planet's bio-health – those we can blame, while remaining intact, even virtuous ourselves…? I think not. Frankenstein's monster exists not only because of Dr. Frankenstein but because of the world that engenders him. Everyone, or pretty well everyone, would agree that global warming is a bad thing; fewer take personal responsibility. Most would agree that race hatred is a bad thing, but few own up to being participants in any way whatsoever. Yet we are all culpable, and that's the theme of my *Comus*. And celebrations come at a cost.

A masque is a play based on dance and music, really. Costumes, stage sets, the long luminous shadow of Inigo Jones, Johnson... Milton's *Comus* was less about these factors than most. It was genre, but went elsewhere, I'd insist. Still, it has many of the ingredients of the masque genre, and it works within those conventions. There's dance here even when the characters are not dancing. The words make the performance in so many ways. It's a work about characters. On one level they are ciphers, but to me they are very real. I've known all these people. I've been some of them, a mixture of them. The unreal bits as much as the real.

What's at stake here? The right to choice, the right of all things to exist without wanton damage and exploitation? Yes, but it's a warped picture the moment we try to qualify and measure it. It's easy to translate Milton's *Comus* into rave culture, into the moral vicissitudes of modern science, into a world of tension between religiosity and consumerism. What's not so easy is to know where this leaves us, as the listeners, the watchers, the readers, the participants. This is a celebration, but what do we ultimately take away from such celebrations?

Landscape is all-important to *Comus*. Mine crosses the wheatbelt of Western Australia and various spaces of Cambridgeshire. These are the places I am most familiar with, and that I write of constantly. They shift between the generic and highly specific – between being there and reading the travel pages. There's a critique of how modernity allows some of us to relate to place. A virtual landscape fused with the one/s we walk through, work in, grew up around. I hope I have created a topological ecology. It's about the geometry of the natural world, our misshaping of it in attempting to profit, aesthetically and commercially to make of it more than is there. The conversion usually brings loss.

This is also a work about gender and sexual politics. About intactness and the roles women get to play in movies – that debate. It's about power and privilege and male inheritance. But nothing is as it seems

So, "Comus" equals revelry. So, the elevation of the Earl of Bridgewater to the President of the Council of Wales and Lord Lieutenant of Wales was the event to trigger Milton's Comus. Bridgewater was relative (son-in-law *and* stepson) to the Countess Dowager of Derby, and the Countess was of the family of the most notorious sex scandal of the age – Lord Castlehaven, related by marriage (to the Countess's daughter), had been executed for his extreme sexual perversities that involved – apart from his wife, his servants, and other parties – his twelve-year-old stepdaughter.

When Milton heard about the possibility of writing a masque, no doubt through Henry Laws, to be performed at Ludlow Castle, all this would have been strongly in his mind as he cast the Earl's two sons and daughter in their roles. Milton biographer A. N. Wilson leaves us in no doubt: "What member of the family, watching Lady Alice have this encounter with her tempter, could fail to remember her cousin Elizabeth, who, so recently, really had been ensnared in the most brutish fashion by her stepfather and his band of monstrous revellers?" Wilson goes on to note that echoing passages that might well allude to such contrasts were edited from the players' copies by Laws. I need not elaborate other than to say that however strongly Milton intended such subtexts, there is a sense of sexual disturbance in the *Comus* that disturbs, even "perverts" the revelries, that brings a triumph of virtue into an ironic and disturbed focus.

Milton's *Comus* is sexually perverse. This is only partially relevant to my rendering, remake, reconfiguring... I use this disturbance as a reflection on the hypocrisy with which we treat the natural world, the environment. Crimes of sexuality, especially against those who have little or no power of refusal, fill the newspapers and television. Wilson calls these public expiations, these show trials, "cleansing rituals", ways of offsetting broader social malaise. The media uses and abuses those with little or no say over their own choices in a way to allure and lure, and reaches fever-point over the legal trials of transgressors while using exploitative material, especially of the young, to sell advertising. The basic sexual hypocrisy is also the hypocrisy of the abuse of the land. The nature documentary is aired while cars, and numerous other consumer products whose creation has been detrimental to the environment, are advertised. The sexualization of the land itself is archetypical and unsurprising, and certainly Milton plays with Greek and Roman traditions as much with those of a pagan English (not Welsh) countryside mediated through Protestantism. This sexualization of the land is ritualistic, and religious. I have interrogated that in the context of exploitation. Milton's *Comus* alludes; I am more direct.

Singing, dance, and ritual. A preserving of the status quo, as the presentation of any art ultimately is, no matter how iconoclastic. Communication is control. But I am writing against that. I think Milton was undermining as much as confirming the powers-that-be. That strange ambivalent relationship with patronage. There are other things going on herein, but I won't over-explain! Suffice it to say, for me poetry and theatre are inseparable, and poetry is a positive ambiguity. And I have always been a fan of genre – maybe, just maybe, *Comus* fits with the horror tradition more than any other. And there are those who celebrate horror with barely a second thought, the medium elevating itself above serious scrutiny.

Cambridge, June 2008

Biographical notes

JOHN MILTON went to school at St. Paul's, the first to teach Greek according to the new Humanism which harnessed rhetoric to the reformation of society. He assimilated this ideal so thoroughly that when at Cambridge he rebelled against what he saw as an outdated university syllabus. For ten years after his BA in 1629 he read independently at his father's house in London, followed by a year's tour of France and Italy, where he delivered papers to academies, collected books and met Galileo. He became the most learned of our major poets, reading in French, Spanish and Hebrew, writing in Latin, Greek and Italian. The arguments he published from *Of Reformation* (1641) onwards were the outcome of this learning, its ideals and impetus, an impetus that carried him into the Civil War (his own brother a Royalist), into regicide and, at the Restoration, to within a hair's breadth of execution. This is his public career.

His poetry runs on a parallel track which never quite meets. His first published poem is a sonnet to Shakespeare in the Second Folio of 1632, while 'A Masque' and 'Lycidas' are similarly contributions to the works of others, incidental to the main work he was preparing. This was to be the fruit of his research into the Arthurian foundation myths of his country, the matter of Britain. It came to grief because his Humanistic training in the critique of sources led him to reject much of that matter as fictitious, and because the momentously current matter of Britain and its reform, indeed salvation, claimed priority.

He was appointed Secretary for the Foreign Tongues in 1649

and wrote for government to the bitter end: *A Ready and Easy Way to Establish a Free Commonwealth* appeared in March 1660. Two months later Milton went into hiding; his books were burned; he was imprisoned; but Parliament ordered his release, Andrew Marvell speaking in his defence. His major works began to emerge seven years later, his matter now the history of God and man. We do not know when he started them.

He died in 1674, the year he published his juvenilia. His father's house, in which he had prepared for his life's task, was destroyed in the Great Fire of 1666.

JOHN KINSELLA's many volumes of poetry include *The Silo: A Pastoral Symphony*, *The Undertow: New and Selected Poems*, *The Hunt*, *Peripheral Light: Selected and New Poems*, *The New Arcadia*, and *Shades of the Sublime & Beautiful*. He is also author of the critical works *Disclosed Poetics: Beyond Landscape and Lyricism* and *Contrary Rhetoric: Lectures on Landscape and Language*. His previous plays are collected as *Divinations: Four Plays*. His other work ranges across genres from short fiction to novels, libretti to autobiography. He is a Fellow of Churchill College, Cambridge University, and a Research Fellow at the University of Western Australia.

TIM CRIBB is a Fellow of Churchill College, Cambridge, where he recently retired as Director of Studies in English and Tutor for Advanced Students. He was an undergraduate at Cambridge, a graduate teaching assistant at the University of Minnesota and a postgraduate at Oxford, where he pursued research on Dickens. Before returning to Cambridge, he was a lecturer at the University of Glasgow.

Throughout the '60s and '70s he acted in summer seasons at the Minack Theatre in Cornwall. During 1977-78 he was seconded as Visiting Senior Lecturer to the University of Ife (Nigeria) where he adapted and directed one of Yeats's plays for the University theatre company. He has directed a number of productions in Cambridge, including plays by Pablo Neruda, Bertolt Brecht, Wole Soyinka and John Kinsella's first play, *Crop Circles* (1998).

Among his other interests are Shakespeare and the Anglophone literature of the Caribbean, especially Wilson Harris and Derek Walcott. He is editor of *Imagined Commonwealths: Cambridge Essays on Commonwealth and International Literature in English* (Macmillan, 1999) and of *The Power of the Word / La Puissance du Verbe* (Rodopi, 2006) and author of *Bloomsbury and British Theatre: the Marlowe Story* (Salt, 2007). He is Senior Treasurer of Cambridge University Marlowe Society.

He is married, with one daughter, and lives in Cambridge.